MW01701978

Happy [illegible] Malcolm!

K+J 1998

Ministry with the Power of Jesus

by Dr. Scott W. Gustafson

Ministry With The Power of Jesus

by

Dr. Scott W. Gustafson

Brunswick Publishing

International Standard Book Number
1-55618-105-1

Library of Congress Catalog Card Number
91-72232

Cover Art by Paula Lind Gustafson

Published in the United States of America

by

Brunswick Publishing Corporation

RT. 1, BOX 1A1
LAWRENCEVILLE, VIRGINIA 23868

For Elca

Table of Contents

Acknowledgements ix

Introduction 1

CHAPTER ONE: THE CHURCH IN THE WORLD............ 13

Jesus' Promises 17

Jesus' Presence and the Transformation of Reality 25

Ambiguity, Presence and Discernment 31

Ambiguity and Grace 37

CHAPTER TWO: THE TASK AND CHARISM OF THE ORDAINED MINISTRY 48

The Ordained and the Task of Discernment............. 49

Ordination as Charism 63

In Defense of Presence... 75

The Charism Ordination Bestows and Other Gifts of the Spirit............................ 81

CHAPTER THREE: PASTORAL AUTHORITY.................. 85

The Power and Authority of Jesus 86

The Authority and Power of the Ordained............. 96

The Ordination of Women 105

Who Shall Be Ordained? 118

CHAPTER FOUR: THE PRIESTHOOD OF ALL BELIEVERS 123

The Ministry of the People of God 124

The Priesthood of All Believers and the Organization of the Body of Christ 135

From Sunday to Monday 148

Endnotes 151

Acknowledgements

This book is a community project, and that means it is different from books that are the result of the deliberation of a committee. A committee project only includes those items which the majority of the committee might agree. A community project is greatly influenced by the community out of which it arises, but one person assumes responsibility for its contents. In my opinion, the work of a theologian is more communal than it is the work of a committee. The theologian is influenced by and in dialogue with many, but ultimately the words are his or her own. Maybe they will later be clarified. Maybe they will later be retracted, but the responsibility for theology remains with the theologian no matter how much the theologian has been influenced by others.

In my case the influence that I have received from other members of the Body of Christ has been tremendous. My parents, Charlotte and Emil Gustafson, allowed me to experience ministry to others and be a recipient of ministry. The congregations with which I have served as a pastor—the Lutheran Church of the Redeemer in McLean, Virginia, and Bethel Lutheran Church in Frederick, Maryland—accorded me example after example of lay ministry. My ordained colleagues, particularly Pastor Iver Haugen, have often demonstrated to me the tasks and charism of the ordained ministry in effective and empowering ways. The students I have taught at the Lutheran Theological Seminary at

Gettysburg and more briefly at the Lutheran Theological Seminary at Philadelphia have helped me achieve more clarity in this project. The pastors I have taught in graduate courses have aided me tremendously. Some of their questions prompted the writing of whole new sections of this study so that the charism that ordination bestows might be stated more clearly. The lay people I have taught in the Lay School of Theology in Gettysburg, Pennsylvania have also encouraged and influenced this effort. Even the Aid Association of Lutherans has helped with a contribution toward the publication of this study.

More specifically, I would like to thank Ruth Gritsch for her helpful suggestions and reading of this manuscript. My words cannot express the degree to which her efforts enhanced the clarity of this project. I do not think that it yet meets her standards, but her suggestions have improved this in many, many ways. I would also like to thank her husband and my friend and colleague Eric Gritsch for his continued support of my efforts. My wife, Brenda Lange-Gustafson, has also aided me in many ways. She read this manuscript and offered suggestions ranging from the fundamental to the typographical, and she has, as always, supported me in my work.

Finally, I would like to thank my sister, Paula Lind Gustafson for designing the cover of this book, and Dr. Walter J. Raymond and his staff at Brunswick Press for the gracious and generous way they have handled the publication of this book.

Introduction

There is something wrong with the Church. Indeed the primary source of unbelief for many people is not an inability to believe in a God, it is the activity of those who call themselves followers of God. Most people can see that the institutional Church normally prefers wealth to poverty. Many know that Christians associate more with the powerful than with the powerless. Some even suspect that our ordained ministers often prefer to be served than to serve. One reason for such miscarriages of the Gospel of Jesus Christ is that Christians generally prefer the authority and power that the world bestows to the authority and power that Jesus gives to His disciples. To complicate matters further, we do not even recognize that there is a profound difference between these two sorts of powers! We do not even notice that the power that the world bestows receives its authority from death, and Jesus gives life. Since the distinction between these two sorts of power is crucial to this presentation, a brief consideration of the characteristics of these two sorts of power is necessary.

The power that receives its authority from death is easiest to describe because it is most familiar. This is the power to kill. This power can manifest itself in the actual termination of the life of another, but it is usually far more subtle than this. Normally the threat of physical death is enough to gain compliance. We cooperate with this power in order to remain physically alive. For example, the threat of death is operative in all attempts to crush the spirit of the living. Indeed it is operative in any attempt to turn a living thing into an object, as can be seen in political oppression and in the destruction of the environment. If a living thing dies it becomes an object. If a man dies while eating dinner at a restaurant, someone else has to deal with his body, and he is not going to help. When he was alive, he could move. He could have helped. But, upon dying, the man became an object that must be moved by another. At the very least, therefore, death is that which turns what was once living into an object.

Most of the time death does not have to kill. Because we prefer a metaphorical death to the real thing, we human beings often cooperate with the power of death by acting like objects so that those who employ death's power will not have to actually kill us. We act like objects so that we will not become objects. We do what we are told. We act as those who exercise death's power wish us to act. We become like pieces of furniture which can be moved at the pleasure of their owner and, in so doing, we cooperate with the power of death.

If this is true, it follows that something as mundane as a corporate memo can be employed by death's power. Such a memo treats those to whom it is written as if they were objects. It may demand attendance at a meeting, but attendance is required so that participants can be informed about what is going to happen to them whether they like it or not. To the extent that this is the case, we cooperate in our own deaths. We allow ourselves to be moved by another, and we do not resist. We are content to do the bidding of another because the other can deprive us of benefits, or even kill us. There are, after all, certain benefits—like money, power and prestige—that can come with cooperating in one's own death.

It is these benefits that make the power and authority of death so attractive and alluring.

Jesus is not intelligible to many people precisely because He does not employ a power that derives its authority from death. We find His unconditional promise of life impossible to understand because we presume death's dominion. How, after all, is it possible for Jesus to rule if He does not threaten us with death? How can He demand obedience if He is unwilling to enforce His will? Those who grant priority to death's dominion have to ask such questions because they can understand the world in no other way. They assume death is God and can see Jesus' power and authority only in so far as it is derived from the power and authority of death.

The good news, of course, is that Jesus receives His power from the Father and not from death. As such, His is the power of life. It is this power of life that Jesus bestows upon His followers. To be sure, Jesus' followers do not often use the power that they have been given, but Jesus bestows this power of life nonetheless.

Forgiveness is one example of the power of life that Jesus bestows, but, unfortunately, very few people recognize its life-giving power. This defect can be quickly remedied by asking questions like, "How many relationships have crumbled due to our inability to forgive?" "How many marriages die because husbands cannot forgive their wives or wives cannot forgive their husbands?" "How many people commit murder because they cannot forgive?" "How many wars have been fought because nations cannot forgive?" On the other hand, "How many marriages live because one spouse can forgive another?" "How many people now live because forgiveness has happened between a husband and a wife?" "How many lives have been saved because one nation has forgiven another?" The power of life itself resides in forgiveness. But even though forgiveness creates life, it is still very difficult to forgive.

The reason forgiving is so difficult stems from its very nature. Contrary to popular expression, forgiving is not forgetting. (If this were the case we would be hard pressed to call a forgiving God omniscient). Forgiving is refusing to insist on your rights.[1] In modern North American culture, we find this very difficult because we often equate our rights with our very lives. The relationship between rights and personhood is very close. Those who do not have rights are legally non-persons, and can be treated like non-entities or property. The law does not protect them. Currently the abortion debate rages in the United States. One of the determinate issues of this debate is whether or not the unborn have legal rights. As long as abortions are legal, the unborn do not have the legal right to live. As long as they lack this right, the government will officially treat the unborn as non-persons. Other illustrations make the same point. In Nazi Germany the government declared that the Jewish people did not have rights, and as a consequence, nearly succeeded in exterminating European Judaism. In the United States, black slaves had few rights and were counted as property instead of as people under the law. The mere mention of these examples not only illustrates the close relationship between rights and personhood, but it also illustrates the close relationship between rights and human life. In this day and age, a person's life is protected by his or her government only to the extent that the person is thought to have rights. If one loses one's rights, one courts death itself. Rights are a protection against death.

If all this is true, our difficulty in forgiving others becomes quite apparent. If forgiving is the refusal to insist on one's rights, and if one's very life is placed in jeopardy by the absence of rights, then the act of forgiving courts death. A person faces the very real possibility of death in not insisting on his or her rights because this action allows the one forgiven to treat the one who forgives as if he or she were dead. The surprise in all this is that in the death that forgiveness courts, new life is a possibility.

The relationship between forgiveness and life as well as our preference for the power of death is illustrated in Matthew 18: 23-35.

> Therefore the Kingdom of heaven may be compared to a king who wished to settle accounts with his servants. When he began the reckoning, one was brought to him who owed him ten thousand talents; as he could not pay, the lord ordered him to be sold, with his wife and children and all that he had, and payment be made. So the servant fell on his knees, imploring him, "Lord, have patience with me, and I will pay you everything." And out of pity for him the lord of that servant released him and forgave him the debt. But that same servant, as he went out, came upon one of his fellow servants who owed him a hundred denarii, and seizing him by the throat he said, "Pay what you owe." So his fellow servant fell down and besought him, "Have patience with me, and I will pay you." He refused and went and put him in prison till he should pay his debt. When his fellow servants saw what had taken place, they were greatly distressed and they went and reported to their lord all that had taken place. Then his lord summoned him and said to him, "You wicked servant. I forgave you all that debt because you asked me; and should not you have mercy on your fellow servant as I had mercy on you?" And in anger his lord delivered him to the jailers, till he should pay all of his debt.

This parable illustrates what has been said so far about forgiveness. In the first place, forgiving is synonymous with refusing to insist on one's rights. The lord had the right to have the servant and his family sold into slavery. No one would have condemned him. He would merely have been doing what was his right to do. The lord, however, did not insist on his rights, and in so doing, he forgave the servant. This act of forgiving demonstrates the second characteristic of forgiveness, namely, its intimate relationship to life. In forgiving his servant, the lord made new life for the servant a possibility. Free from the burden of debt (this debt was close to the equivalent of the National Debt of the United States of America *before* the Reagan administration), the servant could walk in newness of life. Freed from the burden of such debt, the servant could have been an agent of life. He could have given life—in a smaller way—to his fellow servant. He need not have insisted on his rights anymore because his being was already secure in the freedom his lord had given him.

This new situation illustrates another aspect of forgiveness which has yet to be discussed. Simply stated, the power to forgive resides in the fact that we have first been forgiven. We have already discussed how difficult it is to forgive because of forgiveness' close association with death. We have wondered where we get the strength to risk the death that can accompany an act of forgiveness. This parable tells us. We can risk the death that is associated with forgiveness because we have first been forgiven. Moreover, the magnitude of the debt from which we have been released is so great that we can see that our lives are not under the power and dominion of death at all! Rather our lives are in the hands of the one who forgives us. For, the One who died rather than kill now lives and grants us the power to breathe life into hopeless situations. To do so, however, we must employ the power of life that He has given us.

That our employment of the power of life is not a necessary outcome of our being given the power of life is also demonstrated by this parable. The forgiven servant in this parable refuses to employ the power that he has been given, and, as a consequence, finds himself in a prison—perhaps of his own design. (I say this because the punishment that the lord initially intended for the servant was for the servant and his family to be sold as slaves, but the second punishment was to be imprisoned until he should pay his debt. This, after all, was the punishment that the unmerciful servant had designed for the one he refused to forgive).

This prison was a consequence of the man's preference for the authority and power of death instead of life. These may be harsh words, but the situation of this forgiven, yet self-condemned, servant is analogous to the condition of many of our churches in North America. We are the forgiven ones who continue to prefer the authority and power of death to the power of life that forgiveness brings. This preference for death can be seen in our failure in our relationships to the poor. It can be seen in our failure to be good stewards of this planet. It can even be seen in the way we organize our church bodies. Here, our preference for worldly authority is so obvious because our churches adopt power structures that mimic the economic and political power structures of the world. Finally, and surprisingly just as important as the preferences just listed, our preference for the authority and power of death can be seen in how we understand and implement ministry; for, is it not in ministry that those of us who are in authority continue to lord it over those who are not in authority—despite our Lord's warnings to the contrary?[2] Indeed, we *are* the forgiven servant who still prefers death to life!

This preference for death is not a phenomenon unique to this particular generation. It has probably been present throughout the Church history. Even during times when the authority and power of life are most pronounced, the authority and power of death are not too far from the surface. The sixteenth century reformers had the opportunity to reject the authority and power of death in favor of the authority and power of life. Their theologies certainly point in this direction. The principal tenet of the Reformation—justification by faith—was interpreted by many to be both a description of the Gospel of Christ and the infusion of new life into a dying medieval civilization.

It was as a consequence of this message that certain, rather radical proposals such as the notion of the priesthood of all believers were made popular. For the purpose of this study, this notion is notable. In contrast to the medieval doctrines of ordination, which maintained that ordination bestowed a substantial or ontological change on the man who was ordained,[3] the priesthood of all believers maintained that any believer, male or female, is priest, bishop and pope by virtue of baptism. If such a concept is taken seriously, it challenges the very notion of hierarchy (a word which comes from two Greek words for "priest" and "first"); for, how can priests lord it over the people of God if everyone is a priest by virtue of baptism? If such hierarchy persists, it cannot be maintained on the basis of this notion. It must be maintained on the basis of some other sort of rationale.

Indeed, the sixteenth century reformers did not organize in accord with the insights implicit in the doctrines of justification by faith and the priesthood of all believers. With the notable exception of some ecclesiastical bodies of the left wing of the Reformation, the reformers failed to discern their opportunity to organize in accord with the post-Constantinian era that was emerging. Instead, they tried to reestablish Constantinianism. They sought the favor of Princes. They adopted theologies that helped justify existing governments. They organized their churches in a way that was quite similar to the structure of the governments they served. In so doing, the reformers brought their reformation to a halt. They failed to implement their insight that no matter how good or necessary governments might be, the governments of the world operate according to the authority and power of death. By adopting political models for their organizations instead of trying to develop new structures more in accord with the power and authority of life, they continued to incorporate the authority and power of death into the Church's structures. Now, it is true that the Church is in the world. It is also true that in this meantime between the ascension and Jesus' return, the world's preference for death will be difficult to exorcise from the Church, but *this preference for death ought not be placed into the very constitutional structure of our church organizations.*

In order to be faithful, the Church must place itself under a different authority. This authority is the authority and power of the God of life who became flesh in Jesus Christ. A good place to begin to remedy this defect in the way we normally organize ourselves is to take a close look at our teaching on ministry because here the consequences of our preference for the authority and power of death are quite obvious. For example, we have the tendency to describe the power of the ordained ministry in terms of worldly power, and since worldly power is grounded in the authority of death, this supposition demands that those with such power try to turn those who do not have such power into objects. This has happened; it is reflected in the serious gap that now exists between the ordained and other Christians. As it now stands, either the ordained try to lord it over the laity or the laity try to lord it over the ordained. This gap will persist as long as we operate according to death's authority. As long as death rules, the relationship between the ordained and the people of God will be governed by the question, "Who will dominate whom?" Moreover, since death seeks to turn all living things into objects, the only question that the distinction between the ordained and the people of God poses is, "Who is going to be the object of whom?" Will the ordained be the ones who are manipulated by the laity, or will the laity be manipulated and controlled by the ordained?

Indeed, in a Church governed by the power and authority of death, the particular group or persons in question may vary, but the question, "Who is going to be the object?" remains. If the line is drawn between men and women, the question is who will dominate. If the line is drawn between white and black or white and hispanic, the same question is operative. If the line is drawn between homosexual and heterosexual, the question, "Who will be the object?" still remains. Since the authority and power of death is manifested by its ability to turn the living into objects, allegiance to that power pits one person against another. To the extent that a theology of ministry is done against the background of the authority and power of death, it can do nothing else but divide. It will not build up.

The rest of this essay attempts to construct a doctrine of ministry that rejects death's dominion. Since the Church is the foundation of both the ordained and lay ministries, an analysis of the Church in the world will begin this inquiry. Here the Church will be described as an event that happens whenever believers gather where Jesus has promised to be present. Since Jesus is not the same thing as the gathering, but is present in the gathering, the primary objective of believers who gather where Jesus has promised to be present is to discern Jesus' presence, to witness to that presence and follow Jesus. In other words, discernment, witness and discipleship, compose ministry. The difference between the ministry of the ordained and the ministry of the people of God rests in the fact that the ordained normally discern, witness, and follow Jesus in contexts where Jesus has promised to be present, and the people of God more often try to discern, witness and follow Jesus in contexts that Jesus has not promised to be present, but is present nevertheless.

After establishing the necessity for discernment, the next chapter discusses the ordained ministry. Here it will be argued that, like all charisma, the charism that ordination bestows is for the building up and not for the division of the Church. This is, of course, consistent with both the nature of a spiritual gift as St. Paul understands it and the background of the authority and power of life. To reinforce this new background, the third chapter will be devoted to a study of the sort of power and authority that Jesus bestows on His disciples. It is in this context that issues like the ordination of women will be raised.

The final chapter is devoted to the priesthood of all believers. It is my hope that this essay will be so structured that it will be obvious to the reader that the ministry of the whole people of God was being discussed from the beginning. It is, however, specifically dealt with here not because it is last and least important, but because it is in this area that the most important practical claims are made in this presentation. These concern the nature of parish organization as well as ways that the mission of the church in the world can be better supported by our local congregations. It is the contention of this essay that one of the reasons for the perceived gap between Sunday and Monday is that we continue to operate against a background that assumes death's dominion. When this is so, the issue of who dominates whom is paramount, and in many of our churches it is the clergy that dominate the laity. It is here proposed that we begin to understand ministry against the background of the power and authority that Jesus bestows and not the background of the power and authority of death. How this shift might alter our ministries is the subject of what follows.

Chapter One

The Church in the World

The Church is in the world for one simple reason. The world is where her risen Lord chooses to be. As a consequence the Church is not primarily a building though it may need buildings. More surprisingly, the Church is not "the people" though, by God's grace, it contains people. The Church is more of an event or happening than anything else. It happens when believers gather where Jesus, the incarnate Word of God, has promised to be present.[4] Just any gathering of believers does not constitute the Church. As a group of believers gathered to play softball might not be the Church, so a group of clergy gathered to draw up the constitution of a particular denomination's national organization might not be the Church. The existence of the Church depends on the promises of her Lord. Whenever believers gather where Jesus has promised to be, the Church happens. Moreover, whenever believers corporately choose not to gather where Jesus has promised to be present, the Church is indicted. The reality of the Church depends on the promises of her Lord and Savior Jesus Christ. These promises are specific promises that associate Jesus, the Word of God, with specific events.

It is of fundamental importance to a theology of ministry to recognize, and stress from the start, that Jesus can also be present in places where He has not promised to be. Jesus is alive. Jesus is an adult. Jesus can go where he wants. As a matter of fact, one reason believers gather where Jesus has promised to be is so that they will then be more likely to recognize Jesus should they encounter Him where He has not promised to be but is present nonetheless. If I promise to be at a certain event, and you come to meet me there, you are then more likely to recognize me should you encounter me elsewhere. Likewise, if a believer encounters Jesus in a medium in which He has promised to be present, she is more likely to recognize Jesus should she encounter Him in everyday life. Moreover, it is in this distinction between the places where Jesus has promised to be present and the places Jesus has not promised to be but is present nonetheless, that the distinction between the tasks traditionally associated with the ordained ministry and the tasks traditionally associated with the ministry of the whole people of God resides. To put this distinction simply, the ordained attempt to make sure that Jesus' presence in places He has promised to be is as unambiguous as possible so that it will be more likely, rather than less likely, that Jesus will be identified by believers when they encounter Him in everyday life.

It must be stressed from the start that this is a distinction between tasks. It is not compartmentalizing or isolating tasks into ministries appropriate only to the ordained or the laity. In the first place, it will be argued that discerning Jesus' presence in places where He has promised to be is always a corporate action. By its very nature, the attempt to make this presence unambiguous as possible involves conversation within the Body of Christ. Such discernment is the task of all the baptized. In the second place, the reality of the life of the Church informs us that the tasks traditionally associated with the ordained have never been the exclusive domain of the ordained, and the tasks traditionally associated with the laity have never been the exclusive domain of the laity. Lay persons have preached, administered the sacraments, and done all tasks normally associated with the ordained ministry, and ordained persons have worked in factories, led social movements, and in general testified to Jesus' presence in places Jesus has not promised to be but is nevertheless present. Do not let the traditional distinction between the tasks of the ordained and the people of God undermine the historical fact that no task is the exclusive domain of either. Finally, the faithful activity of Christians is always the same in principle even though varied contexts lead to different actions. Whether we are where we believe Jesus has promised to be present or elsewhere, our task is always to discern Jesus' presence, to testify to that presence and to follow as disciples.

Since discernment, witness and discipleship define ministry, a brief description of them is in order. The character of discernment is best illustrated by the parables of the Hidden Treasure and the Pearl of Great Price.[5] In both parables, the person finds something in an unlikely place and dedicates his life to the acquisition of that which has been found. One's life is ordered by that which is discerned. Like the scientist who must order her experiments in a manner consistent with the solution which she has only dimly perceived, a woman who is attempting to discern Jesus, where Jesus is present, must order her life in a manner consistent with Jesus. The agenda of the one who discerns is informed by that which is to be discerned. As the man who found the treasure in the field must do certain things in order to acquire the field, so those attempting to discern Jesus must act in accord with that which they wish to discern. If Jesus is being discerned, only agendas that are appropriate to the discernment of Jesus can be used. The only difference between discernment in these parables or even in scientific experimentation and the character of discernment that this essay wishes to convey is that the process of discernment is usually more corporate than these parables and examples indicate.

Witness is best described through the character of John the Baptist as the Gospel of John seems to portray him. In this Gospel, John the Baptist's witness appears to be twofold. First, he makes no claim about himself or his own powers. "He confessed, he did not deny, but confessed, 'I am not the Christ.' " John the Baptist then goes on to say that he is nothing but " . . . the voice of one crying in the wilderness, Make straight the way of the Lord, . . ."[6] The second characteristic of witness that John the Baptist illustrates is that of merely pointing to Jesus. Jesus walks by John, and John points to Jesus saying, "Behold, the Lamb of God." Immediately, John's own disciples follow Jesus. John's (movement) diminishes while Jesus' following increases because of the nature of John's own testimony. John is the one who most adequately points away from himself and toward the living reality of Jesus in the Gospel of John. He is not a disciple because he does not follow. Instead, he is the embodiment of a true witness because he deflects all praise and glory from himself to Jesus. He gets himself out of the way so that the one to whom he witnesses might be seen.

Discipleship is nothing less than following Jesus. One of the clearest expressions of this is Mark 8:27-33. This is the rather familiar story about Jesus asking His disciples, "Who do people say that I am?" His disciples tell Him that some people say that He is John the Baptist and others say He is Elijah or another of the prophets. Then Jesus asks, "Who do you say that I am?" To this Peter says, "You are the Christ." The text's view of discipleship is revealed in what happens next. Jesus tells His disciples that He is going to have to suffer and die. Peter then took Jesus aside (the Greek may read that Peter took Jesus aside as a parent would take aside a misbehaving child) and began to rebuke Him, but Jesus rebuked Peter saying, "Get behind me, Satan! For you are not on the side of God, but of men." In this passage Peter, the disciple, seeks to stand in front of His Lord. He tries to establish Jesus' agenda. Jesus reminds Peter that a disciple that ceases to follow is no longer a disciple. Peter is equated with Satan in this passage because Satan is another who seeks to establish Jesus' agenda. A disciple cannot take the lead. The disciple is the one who follows.[7]

Discernment, witness, and discipleship have one important characteristic in common. All those who discern, witness, and follow operate according to the agenda of another. When one discerns, one's agenda is dictated by that which one is attempting to discern. Likewise, the one who witnesses acts in accord with the agenda of the one to whom the witness is directed. Our witness is undermined to the extent that we stand in the way of the one to whom we witness. Discipleship is not unlike witness and discernment in this respect. The disciple does not know where the teacher is going. He or she can only speculate. As long as the disciple remains a disciple, all that the disciple can do is follow. The disciple's life is in the hands of the master.

JESUS' PROMISES

Even where Jesus has promised to be, Jesus' presence is not easy to discern because Jesus never presents Himself outside a medium of some sort. A medium is something in which something else is contained. It differs from a package, however, in that what is contained in a package can be removed, the contents isolated from the package, and the package discarded. A medium is far more intimately related to that which it contains than is a package. Like the medium in which a biologist might grow bacteria, the contents of a medium are often dependent on their particular medium for their survival. If bacteria growing in media are removed from their media, the bacteria die. Living bacteria cannot, therefore, be studied outside their media. In order to study living bacteria, the scientist must discern the bacteria within the media in which they live. This is how it is with Jesus. In order to witness to Jesus, Jesus must be discerned within the medium in which He presents Himself. That is to say that Christians must make every effort to distinguish Jesus from the medium in which He is present without removing Him from the medium, for whenever Jesus is removed from the medium, the incarnation is lost. On the other hand, if Jesus is not distinguished from the medium in which He is present, idolatry is the result because the medium is mistaken for God.

The implication that Jesus' presence depends on certain media may be disconcerting to some, but several examples from the Church's tradition reinforce the validity of the assertion that Jesus never presents Himself apart from a medium of some sort. First, the Trinitarian controversy itself actually concluded that God is a community of three persons. If this is a fair interpretation, it follows that Jesus' being depends on this community, and since a community is a medium (it is something in which something else is contained), it follows that being in a medium may be what it is to be God.

Second, many of the early heresies were heresies precisely because they attempted to remove Jesus from one medium or another. Gnosticism and docetism, for example, tried to remove Jesus from the media of history and humanity. They were deemed heresies by the Church because removing Jesus from media such as these undermined a fundamental assumption of the Gospel, namely, that God is present with humanity in the world in Jesus Christ. If Jesus is removed from such media, the Gospel is undermined.

Finally, and closely related, there is an intimate association between grace and presence in a medium. In other words, if we lose Jesus' presence in a medium, we lose the possibility of grace. Since an entire section will be devoted to this very argument near the end of this chapter, this will not be discussed further here. These three possibilities are merely designed to show that it is possible that some rather profound reasons exist for Jesus' insistence on presenting Himself in certain media.

There are a number of media in which Jesus has promised to be present. Like many of the Reformation's confessional documents, the Augsburg Confessions suggest a couple when it describes the Christian Church as " . . . nothing else than the assembly of all believers among whom the Gospel is preached in its purity and the Holy Sacraments are administered according to the Gospel."[8] Assuming, for now, that the Reformers thought Jesus present in Word and Sacrament, such descriptions of the Church maintain that the Church happens when believers gather (assemble) where Jesus has promised to be present. When believers gather around bread and wine, the preached Word, and when people are incorporated into Jesus' Body through baptism, the Church happens. Such is the important legacy of the churches of the Lutheran and Reformed traditions.

Despite this legacy, these churches may not have given as complete a description of the Church as possible, because they did not recognize other places where Jesus has promised to be present.[9] Using the parable of the Great Judgment found in Matthew 25:31-46, for example, liberation theologians have used the phrase, "Truly I say to you, as you did it to one of the least of these my brothers and sisters, you did it to me," to demonstrate their contention that Jesus has promised to be present with "the least of these." They assert that since this is the case, believers should gather in the midst of "the least of these." While it is true that this might be interpreted differently and that many have disagreed with the liberation theologians' interpretation of this text, such disagreement should not obscure the fact that this has been proposed by faithful Christians as one medium (perhaps the most fundamental medium) in which Jesus has promised to be. Christians, however, have often disagreed concerning the media in which Jesus has promised His presence as well as the character of these media. For example, the debate between Luther and Zwingli over Christ's real presence in the Lord's Supper can easily be described as an unresolved disagreement between Christians concerning the validity of the Lord's Supper as a medium in which Jesus has promised to be present. Zwingli maintained that Jesus could not be present in the Lord's Supper because Jesus was at the right hand of the Father, and since it was physically impossible for a body to be present in two places at once, Jesus could not be present in the Supper. It was for this reason that Zwingli maintained that when Jesus said, "This is my body," He actually meant, "This signifies my body," and, therefore, was not present in the Lord's Supper. Luther, on the other hand, took Jesus' promise literally, even though he too might have believed a body cannot be in two places at once. But, when it came to a conflict between Luther's physics and Jesus' word, Luther chose to believe Jesus' word. Those who side with Luther in this debate, however, are usually quite unwilling to say that those siding with Zwingli are not Christians. They might say that the faith of the Zwinglians is handicapped by an understanding of the Lord's Supper that prevents the intentional appropriation of the benefits of this sacrament, but they would still maintain that those in agreement with Zwingli are Christians. To be sure, there are disagreements about the scope of Jesus' promises, but these disagreements happen within the faith. As a result, the fact that brothers and sisters in Christ disagree about where Jesus has promised to be present does not undermine the description of the Church as an event that occurs whenever believers gather where Jesus has promised to be present.

If disagreements between Christians concerning the specific media in which Jesus has promised to be present do not undermine this description of the Church, it follows that other sorts of media might now be uncritically proposed. The following are possibilities only. Each is subject to debate among the faithful. The only thing that needs to be said is that the Church loses much more if it fails to identify a medium of Christ's presence than it does if it mistakenly identifies such a medium. In the case of Luther's debate with Zwingli, for example, if Zwingli is right, the consequences for Luther are not that severe. Luther merely has believed that Jesus has promised to be somewhere and Jesus has not been there. Some time has been wasted, and that's about all.[10] Moreover, if one also notes that Jesus *can* be present where He has not promised to be, the consequences of such an error are even less severe.

If Zwingli is wrong, however, Zwingli cannot intentionally appropriate the power that the presence of the Lord bestows in the Supper. To be sure, Jesus is present whether or not His presence is acknowledged, but we cannot make use of Jesus' availability to us if we do not recognize this possibility. In addition, if we deny Jesus' presence from the start, we might disregard the commands of our Lord which identify the medium in which He has promised to be present. If Jesus' commands are disregarded, The Supper could become any old meal—and Jesus has not promised to be present at any old meal. When He says, "Do this . . . ." Jesus is promising to be present at meals where "this" is done. Disregarding such commands may be more detrimental than our failure to appropriate Jesus' presence. We could so alter the event that the commands of Jesus are not being obeyed, and, as a consequence, there would be no promises associated with the event.

With this caution concerning acceptance or rejection of a possible medium of Christ's presence in mind, we now turn to some possible media in which Jesus has promised to be present. The following list is not intended to be complete. It is intended to be illustrative.

The first illustration is found in the context of a passage dealing with hierarchical power in the Gospel of Mark. Mark 9:36, 37 says, "And He took a child, put him in the midst of them; and taking him in His arms He said to them, 'Whoever receives one such child in my name receives me, and whoever *receives me*, receives not me but Him who sent me.' " Here Jesus seems to be promising to be present in an event in which a child is received in His name. How one actually receives a child in His name is not discussed. Other things also remain unclear, such as what exactly constitutes a child, but these ambiguities do not undermine the very real possibility that just as Jesus promised to be bodily present in the Lord's Supper when He said, "This is my body," Jesus has promised His presence whenever a child is received in His name.

The second medium in which Jesus has promised His presence is discussed in Matthew 18:15-20. This passage is about excommunicationing and the disciplining individual Christians. It ends with this promise. "For where two or three are gathered in my name, there am I in the midst of them." This too can be interpreted in a variety of ways. Some may restrict this promise to matters of Church discipline saying that Jesus promises to be present when two or more are gathered in His name for the purposes of Church discipline.

Others might argue that Jesus' promise, "For wherever two or three are gathered in my name, there I am in the midst of them," was used in other contexts prior to Matthew, and that Matthew quoted the saying in context of Church discipline. In that case, this passage might refer to Jesus' promises to be present whenever two or three gather in His name without taking into consideration the activity of the gathering (although gathering in Jesus name excludes some activities). In any case, what we have here is a promise of Jesus that is neither more nor less problematic than more familiar promises like, " . . . this is my body."

Another possible medium in which Jesus has promised to be present, if Scripture is to be believed, is identified in Matthew's apostolic commission. "And Jesus came and said [to His disciples], 'All authority in heaven and on earth has been given to me. Go therefore and make disciples of all nations, baptizing them in the name of the Father, and of the Son and of the Holy Spirit, teaching them to observe all I have commanded you; and lo, I am with you always, to the close of the age.' "[11] While certain interpretations of this text find no link between the promise of presence Jesus makes here and the actual activities of the apostles, another interpretation might say that the acts the apostles are commanded to perform in this passage are the media in which Jesus is promising to be present. Such an interpretation would indicate that when, in the spirit of the apostles, people go on missions to all nations, where they are baptizing and teaching all that Jesus has commanded them, then Jesus is present. Here mission, teaching, and baptizing into the Triune name become media in which Jesus has promised to be.

These are a few of the media in which it is at least conceivable that Jesus has promised to be present; and when believers gather in places where Jesus has promised to be present, the Church happens. This is how the Church exists in the world. This is how the Church incarnates herself around her incarnate Lord. Moreover, all people seem to know that gathering in places Jesus has promised to be present is what the Church is supposed to be doing.

When the visible, institutional church is indicted by Christians and non-Christians alike, she is indicted because of her refusal to go where Jesus has promised to be present. Knowing that our Lord is among "the least of these," the institutional church normally prefers to remain in the presence of the powerful. Knowing that the one who receives a child in Jesus' name receives Jesus, the institutional church normally ignores the young who often find no place for themselves in our churches. Knowing that she has been commanded to proclaim Christ to all nations, the institutional church prefers to discuss the ground of being or something else that she thinks she holds in common with other faiths, when all along many of the people of other faiths are more interested in what we have to say about Jesus.[12]

It is often true that those outside the institutional church indict her for not frequenting the media in which Jesus has promised to be present. This fact adds more validity to the description of Church as what happens whenever believers gather in media in which Jesus has promised to be, because it is a relatively accurate description of how the world understands the role of the Church in the world. Non-believers seem to know what we ought to be, and they often accuse us of not being what we should be and claim to be. To say that non-believers understand more about us than we sometimes understand of ourselves is hardly inconsistent with our heritage. Like the fellow servants who told their lord of the lack of compassion of the unmerciful servant in the parable discussed in the introduction, those who are not aware of God's grace still testify against the Church. They know unfaithfulness when they see it even though they may not as yet be called.

JESUS' PRESENCE AND THE TRANSFORMATION OF REALITY

> For as the rain and snow come down from heaven and return not thither but water the earth making it bring forth and sprout giving seed to the sower and bread to the eater so shall my word be that goes forth from my mouth it shall not return to me empty but it shall accomplish that which I purpose and prosper in the thing for which I sent it.[13]

God's Word does something. It shows reality to be other than it appears. It transforms the ones who appropriate this newness, and it judges those who do not. Jesus is the Word of God. Where Jesus is present, reality can be understood quite differently. All of the media in which Jesus has promised to be present transform reality and demand that reality be interpreted quite differently. If we refuse to grasp this new reality, Christian life and ministry will be severely handicapped.

A short, personal story illustrates the transforming power of Jesus' presence in places He has promised to be. My wife Brenda and I have tried to have a "modern marriage" for the fifteen years of wedded bliss we have shared. By "modern marriage" I do not mean what some mean by "open marriage." I mean that we have created the illusion that we have abolished the typical sexual role stereotypes of our predecessors. Brenda was the first to get her Ph.D., for example. I helped support her. She then helped to support me in my education. We both clean house, though she does this more than I do (this is truly a modern marriage). We both wash dishes and prepare meals, though she is now doing this far more frequently than I. I admit that I still long for the days of old when men were only required to do "man" things like spit and lift heavy objects while women did all of the dirty work, but I try, sometimes not very hard, to repent of those former ways.

When we were blessed with children, we decided we would divide up child care as much as possible. At night we would share the responsibilities. We started out alternating. First she would get up with the crying baby. Next I would, but later we decided that it would be easier if we divided the night into two parts. One of us would be responsible for crying children from 11:00 pm. to 3:00 am., and the other would be responsible from 3:00 am to 7:00 a.m. I will admit, publicly, that this too was not a completely equal arrangement, because when she would wake up for her shift, she would generally do so as quietly as possible, but my own sinfulness tempted me to let her know I was awake, and I often succumbed to that temptation. Another reason the arrangement was not completely equal was the fact that I could choose the shift I desired, and I chose my shift with ruthless calculation. Such calculation got me into trouble one night. This night I figured I had it made. According to my calculations, our son Gregory had been sleeping for five hour periods. He had gone to sleep at around 9:10 pm. He was sure to wake up between 2:00 am. and 2:30 am. I knew this!!! Moreover, if Brenda got him back to sleep by 3:00 am., I could count on a full night's sleep! With joy and cunning I chose the late shift on this fateful night.

I was so confident of my choice that evening that I stayed up a little later. I watched a little T.V., and I went to bed around 1:00 am. I was awakened at 3:05 a.m. by the crying of my son. I felt betrayed. He had slept almost six hours, and it was now my turn to deal with him. I got up, but not without complaint. I warmed up a bottle. I fed him. I had more trouble than normal getting him back to sleep, but I did so by 3:50 a.m.

and crept back into bed. He awakened once more at 3:59 a.m. During that nine minute period I had managed to fall asleep. I woke up once again. I got him out of his crib. He wanted to play! I finally got him back to sleep at 4:50 am. Again, I had just drifted off into slumber land when Gregory was crying again. Again, I got him. Again, I got him back to sleep. Again, he awakened. I was getting angry. I was beginning to understand child abuse. I was ready to throw this kid through the wall. It was then—by the power of the Holy Spirit no doubt—that I recalled a text on which I was supposed to preach in the near future. It was Mark 9:33-37 which includes the verse, "Whoever receives one such child in my name receives me; and whoever receives me receives not me but Him who sent me." It was at this point that my relationship to my son was transformed. The facts of this relationship were still the same. My son had done few positive things to "earn" my love. He had thrown up on me, urinated on me, and kept me awake at night. These acts do not increase your value as a human being by the standards of the world. But that promise of Jesus transformed our relationship because that very promise granted my son what Helmut Thielicke calls an "alien dignity." My son has a dignity, not because of what he has done, but because of the One who accompanies him when he is received in Jesus' name. This promise transforms one activity that is vital to human life, namely, parenting, and it may have implications, beyond parenting, for the strained relationship between the sexes. The labor involved in child rearing may well be one of the reasons for patriarchy. Raising children can be a dirty, thankless task. Since there is no glory in it, it is natural for those who can avoid it, to avoid it; and men are the ones who can usually avoid it without killing the child outright. Traditionally, men have not only avoided this task, they have made the avoidance of the task into a virtue. In the text we are discussing, for example, Jesus was risking His credibility as a teacher and as a respectable man by taking the child in His arms. No "respectable" man would stoop to such an indignity in first century Palestine. In any case, Jesus' promise transforms parenting. Not only does it open possibilities for mothers and fathers, but, if an assembly of believers actually accepted children in the name of Jesus, the whole congregation would find itself accepting parental responsibilities. If we would understand such a ministry to be part of our mission, the stress and isolation felt by parents in our modern nuclear families, as well as the stress and isolation that is doubly felt by single parents, would definitely be reduced in the Body of Christ and even throughout the world.

Similar transformations can occur if we appropriate other media in which Jesus has promised to be present. The context of the Church's mission would be dramatically altered if the Church took seriously Jesus' promise to be present in mission. Jesus' promise to be with us to the close of the age when we "go to all nations . . . " may well indicate that when disciples engage in missionary activity, they find that Jesus is already there in the mission field. In this case, the task of the disciple would be to discern Jesus' presence in the place to which they have been sent, to witness to that presence and to follow. This is quite different from what we have often done. Traditionally we have operated under the false assumption that missionaries are the ones who bring Jesus to places He has never been. We have failed to recognize that Jesus often goes before us into these locales. In any case, if Jesus is present but undiscerned in the mission field, it follows that the discernment of Jesus involves the attempt to distinguish Jesus from the culture in which He has incarnated Himself. This means that we cannot disregard the cultural context of the mission field. Accordingly, we will be less likely to confuse

Christianity with the culture from which we have been sent. If we assume that Jesus is already present in the place we are being sent, and if we understand our role to be the discernment of Jesus' presence in that culture, we must take the culture of the place to which we are sent very seriously indeed; for only by doing so will we be able to distinguish Jesus from the medium in which He presents Himself.

Another problem that is promoted by the belief that missionaries bring Jesus to non-Christians, and do not find Jesus in the midst of non-Christians, is the paternalistic attitude of the missionaries that we have had in the past and now seek to avoid. If we think we bring Jesus, we cannot avoid thinking that we have something that others might appropriate. If, on the other hand, we acknowledge that Jesus has gone before us into this place and has been with the people all along, such paternalism is less likely, and it is then possible for a missionary to be a student of those who will teach her. The relationship between the missionary and the people to whom she ministers depends more on the give and take of conversation than on unilateral, one way communication. The missionary needs to incorporate into her own life the stories, rituals, and language of those to whom she has been sent in order to have a chance to distinguish Jesus from the culture; the people to whom the missionary is sent need to hear the reality of their culture interpreted as a part of God's story on earth.

Finally, taking seriously Jesus' promise to be present when we " . . . go to all nations . . . " alters our dialogues with other religions of the world. Currently, these dialogues seem to be at the rather sticky phase where we Christians do not want to discount the reality of the religious experiences of other faiths, but, at the same time, insist on the uniqueness of our own heritage. How might we approach our conversations with other religions with respect for their heritage and experience, and yet insist that Jesus is the way, the truth and the life? The openness demanded by such a situation is quite impossible to achieve if we believe that we bring Jesus into such a situation. If, however, we cling to the promise that Jesus is already present when we go to all nations, we will come to understand that our task in the dialogue is to discern the places where we think our Lord is already present and to witness to what is already there. This means, of course, a reinterpretation of the other religion. But, in this reinterpretation, it is essential that we not deny the facts of that religion as they are presented to us. Those who are engaged in such dialogue must realize that there are a variety of ways to interpret the facts of life. A Christian must only insist that interpretations be faithful to the Lordship of Christ. It is true that our interpretation of these facts may well be different from their own interpretations, allowing them to understand themselves differently, but the reverse is also true. They will interpret our facts, feelings, and thoughts differently, so that we may also see ourselves differently. What more can one expect from a conversation?

Another transformation occurs if "the least of these" in Matthew 25:40 is appropriated as a medium in which Jesus has promised to be present. Since Biblical times, Christians have attempted to discuss the Christian life in ways that do not undermine God's activity in salvation. In the process, we have raised the question of the relationship between faith and works. But, if "the least of these" is a medium in which Jesus has promised to be present, going to "the least of these" is no more a good work than is taking part in Holy Communion. One goes to the Lord's Supper and to "the least of these" to receive something. Both are "for you." In both cases, we are in the presence of Jesus.

Moreover, since we go to the least of these in order to be in the presence of our Lord, we do not go to them in order to minister to them (though that may happen). We go to receive ministry. This may sound strange, but the fact of the matter is that the rich benefit from the ministry of the marginalized more than the marginalized benefit from the rich. One thing presence among "the least of these" does is to draw you out of yourself. It is difficult to be self-absorbed when you are feeding people in a soup kitchen. Indeed, a friend of mine recognized this long ago and continues to use Jesus' presence among "the least of these" in his pastoral care to some people who he thinks are self-absorbed or moderately depressed. In his opinion, the people he sends among "the least of these" receive more than they give. Could this be because Jesus is there?

The recognition and appropriation of Jesus' presence among "the least of these," like the recognition and appropriation of Jesus' presence in mission, has a transforming effect; and the faithful are handicapped if media such as these go unacknowledged. We are currently so handicapped in our missionary activities, in our social action and in our care and nurture of the young. It is a shame, because it need not be this way. Recognizing Jesus' presence in media such as mission, "the least of these," and the reception of children in His name pushes us beyond what we are and enables us to be the lights to the world that our Lord intends us to be.

AMBIGUITY, PRESENCE AND DISCERNMENT

The scheme that has been articulated so far requires constant discernment on our part. This stems from the nature of the media in which Jesus is incarnated. It is now time to emphasize, as strongly as possible, that even in the places where Jesus has promised to be present, it is not always obvious where Jesus is in these media. For example, God's Word is not always all that clear in a sermon because Jesus is not the sermon. Jesus is present in the sermon. Jesus works salvation in the sermon, but Jesus is not the sermon. The believers who gather must try to discern Jesus' presence in the sermon, and there is no guarantee that they will do so. This does not, of course, mean that the salvation of the believer is dependent on the accurate discernment of Jesus. It does, however, mean that a believer cannot intentionally appropriate Jesus' presence and power for ministry unless Jesus is discerned. God gives us salvation through Jesus' presence, and we, in turn, can best minister in the world by discerning Jesus' presence.

In any case, Jesus is never synonymous with the medium in which He presents Himself. Jesus is not "the least of these." Jesus is present in the midst of the "least of these."Jesus is not the child. Jesus is present when a child is received in His name. Jesus is not the mission of the Church. Jesus is present when believers "Go to all nations . . . ." Believers must constantly discern Jesus in the media in which Jesus presents Himself, and there is no guarantee that even the most faithful effort will be totally accurate in discerning Him.

Even in what some take to be the least ambiguous place where Jesus has promised to be present, the Lord's Supper, there is much ambiguity. Jesus' statement, "This is my body," is certainly one example of such ambiguity. To what does the word "this" refer? Roman Catholics have traditionally interpreted the word "this" quite unambiguously. "This" refers to the elements of bread and wine. On the other hand, Protestants have usually maintained the ambiguity of the word "this." Modern Protestants who maintain Christ's real presence, in particular, often hold that Jesus is really present in the Supper, but they are not so sure of His whereabouts. Jesus may well be in the elements, but He might be present in the midst of the gathering. The entire event with its prayers, motions and gestures could also constitute His body. The same ambiguities are present in the phrase, "This cup is the new covenant in my blood . . . ." What about the fact that many of our gatherings say, "*This* cup . . . ," raise one cup and employ four cups in the distribution of communion? What is the difference between using four chalices and using one hundred tiny pre-filled glasses? I do not intend to answer these questions. I simply use them to demonstrate the fact that even in the medium many take to be the least ambiguous of the media in which Jesus has promised to be present, ambiguity and confusion abound.

All the questions just raised, as well as all questions generated by other media in which Jesus has promised His presence, require us to distinguish Jesus from the medium in which He presents Himself, and we do so as corporately as we can, because the Church gets its best ideas and makes its best observations when it does things as a body. It is only as a body that all of the spiritual gifts we corporately hold can be focused on a particular problem. The Church should indeed have quotas on her committees, but these quotas should be based on spiritual gifts. It would be quite a different meeting if the financial committee of a national or local church could not function until the one with the gift of tongues was present.

No matter what gifts are present at a particular gathering, it is still very difficult to discern Jesus even in media in which He has promised to be present. First, Jesus is not the medium; second, discernment is a corporate event. But it is even more complicated. Jesus, as we have mentioned and now proclaim, is alive!! Whatever else being alive might mean, one thing it means is that Jesus can move. This means that today Jesus might not be in the same exact place where He was discerned yesterday, though He will remain in the medium in question if He has promised to do so. The fact that Jesus is alive might also mean that He might not be doing the same thing in that medium that He was doing yesterday. Paul seems to be making this point in I Corinthians 11:17-29.

But in the following instructions I do not commend you, because when you come together it is not for the better but the worse. For, in the first place, when you assemble as a church, I hear that there is division among you; and I partly believe it, for there must be factions among you in order that those who are genuine among you may be recognized. When you eat together, it is not the Lord's Supper that you eat, for in eating, each one goes ahead with his own meal, and one is hungry and the other is drunk. What? Do you not have houses to eat and drink in? Or do you despise the church of God and humiliate those who have nothing? What shall I say to you? Shall I commend you in this? No, I will not.

For I received from the Lord what I also delivered to you, that the Lord Jesus Christ on the night when he was betrayed took bread, and when he had given thanks, he broke it, and said, 'This is my body which is given for you. Do this in remembrance of me.' In the same way also the cup, after supper saying, 'This cup is the new covenant in my blood; Do this as often as you drink it, in remembrance of me.' For as often as you eat this bread and drink the cup, you proclaim the Lord's death until He comes.

Whoever, therefore, eats the bread or drinks the cup of the Lord in an unworthy manner will be guilty of profaning the body and blood of the Lord. Let a person examine himself (or herself) and so eat of the bread and drink of the cup. For anyone who eats and drinks without discerning the body eats and drinks judgment upon himself (or herself).

The first thing to note is that the Lord's Supper is, for both Paul and the Corinthians, a medium of Jesus' presence. The Corinthians, however, interpret this presence far more unambiguously than Paul. They seem to believe that their salvation is guaranteed because they have the Eucharist at their disposal. Like those living in the last days of the kingdom of Judah, who thought no foreign power could prevail against them because their blessed Jerusalem had the Temple of the Lord, the Corinthians thought that they were secure because they took part in the Lord's Supper. Needless to say, Paul disagreed. Indeed, Paul still maintained that Jesus was present in the Lord's Supper, but He was present for purposes other than edification. Jesus was present in the Corinthian Eucharist for the purpose of judgment. Why? The Corinthians had failed to discern the body. Perhaps they had failed to look for Jesus in the poor among them, and since that was where Jesus was present in this particular gathering, the Corinthians could not discern Jesus.

It is important that the theme of this discussion not prevent us from seeing the possible implications of this text for the situation facing the modern Church. We Christians in North America live in a global community and are members of a global Church. After we eat and drink at our Lord's Table, many of us go out and have the largest meal of the week. We forget that for many of our brothers and sisters throughout the world, the bread and wine they receive in the Lord's Supper may well be the only food they get all day. As a consequence, we must ask if we too take this Supper to our judgment! If so, what can we do? How can we discern the Body? How might we alter our rituals so that we may better understand what Jesus is doing in our midst when we eat and drink His body and blood?

Remarkably, such talk about alterations in our ritualistic expression of the Lord's Supper brings up what ought to be the point of liturgical change. The only justification for a liturgical change within a medium in which Jesus has promised His presence is that, in the opinion of the assembly of believers, Jesus has moved from where He once was, or is now doing something different from what He once did in the medium being considered. When I was growing up, the churches in which I worshipped conducted Holy Communion by having us come to the altar rail, kneel in a line, and wait to receive a paper-like host and a small glass of wine. What was stressed about communion at the time was the individual forgiveness of sins that we received through Holy Communion. This interpretation of the sacrament is not wrong. Holy Communion does involve the forgiveness of individual sins, and the action in those liturgies of my youth reflected such forgiveness. Today, the community in which I most often worship emphasizes the corporate dimensions of Holy Communion. When we gather, we form a circle around a table. We stand facing each other, and, since the circle is continuous, we never lose sight of our neighbors. This too is not wrong. Holy Communion also involves Jesus' presence in the horizontal aspects of Christian communal life. The question that must be addressed in issues of liturgical change and innovation normally is, therefore, not a question about doing a particular liturgy "wrong" at one time and "right" at another. More often than not, the question concerns the discernment of Jesus within the medium of the Lord's Supper. The character that our liturgy takes ought to be influenced by where we have discerned Jesus to be and by what we have discovered Him to be doing.

It has been demonstrated that, if the Church happens when believers gather in media in which Jesus has promised to be present, the result is ambiguity. Moreover, in an age in which we strive to eliminate ambiguity altogether, the recognition of such ambiguity may prove to be all the more uncomfortable. Nevertheless, there are some very positive things that ambiguity promotes. We ought not let our discomfort with ambiguity prevent us from understanding its positive, life-giving features. It is to the task of exploring these features that we now turn.

AMBIGUITY AND GRACE

One of the characteristics of Jesus that bothers many of us is that Jesus never seems to answer a question directly. When asked if a person should pay taxes, Jesus says, "Give me a coin," and institutes a dialogue that culminates in the famous statement, "Render unto Caesar the things that are Caesar's and unto God the things that are God's." He leaves it up to His hearers to figure out what are Caesar's things and what are God's things. Likewise, when He is asked, "Who is my neighbor?" He tells the story about the Good Samaritan, and He leaves His hearers to figure out who their neighbors are. Even Jesus' miracles were ambiguous to the people who witnessed them. Some said He accomplished them by the power of the prince of the demons. Others thought He did so because He was the Messiah, and we all know the variety of ways His disciples and the people interpreted His Messiahship.

It is probably owing to our desire to be in control that we human beings are quite uncomfortable with such ambiguity. Our discomfort, however, leads us to miss the beauty of ambiguity. This beauty can be demonstrated by a theory that has been developed concerning Jesus' parables. At one time many Biblical scholars suggested that the parables of Jesus had one, and only one, meaning; and if we got this meaning, we would understand the parable. In contrast, many people now think that it is quite likely that no one—may be not even Jesus—knew the meaning of the parables. The reason for this assertion is that the parables held in common by Matthew,

Mark, and Luke are seldom if ever interpreted in the same way by the evangelists themselves. This leads one to the conclusion that there never actually was a consensus on these matters. Moreover, it is apparent that sometimes even the evangelist himself does not know how to interpret a particular parable. Take Luke 16:1-13, a text that preachers often plan vacations around, as an example.

> He also said this to His disciples, "There was a man who had a steward, and charges were brought to him that this man was wasting his goods. And he called him and said to him, 'What is this that I hear about you? Turn in the account of your stewardship, for you can no longer be a steward.' And the steward said to himself, 'What shall I do, since my master is taking the stewardship away from me? I am not strong enough to dig, and I am ashamed to beg. I have decided what to do, so that people will receive me into their houses when I am put out of my stewardship.' So summoning his master's debtors one by one, he said to the first, 'How much do you owe my master?' He said, 'A hundred measures of oil.' And he said to him, 'Take your bill and sit down quickly and write fifty.' Then he said to another, 'And how much do you owe?' He said, 'A hundred measures of wheat.' He said, 'Take your bill and write eighty.' The master commended the dishonest steward for his shrewdness."

When interpreting any saying of Jesus it is always important to remember that quotation marks had not been invented when the Bible was written. This means that if a particular text has quotation marks, they are interpretations that tell us that in the opinion of the translator, Jesus is now speaking. In my opinion, the actual parable Jesus told ends with, "The master commended the dishonest steward for his shrewdness," and the rest of what remains in quotation marks, and is actually attributed to Jesus by our translators, may actually be Luke's effort to make sense of this rather strange and surprising parable. Luke may have tried to explain this parable in the following ways;

> . . . for the sons of this world are more shrewd in dealing with their own generation than the sons of light.
>
> And I tell you, make friends for yourselves by means of unrighteous mammon, so that when it fails they may receive you into the eternal habitation.
>
> He who is faithful in a very little is faithful also in much; and he who is dishonest in a very little is dishonest also in much. If then you have not been faithful in that which is another's, who will give you that which is your own?
>
> No servant can serve two masters; for either he will hate one and love the other, or he will be devoted to the one and despise the other. You cannot serve God and mammon.

In his own effort to make sense of this strange and surprising parable, Luke seems to have brought to bear every cliché that is remotely related to the subject matter. If he had gone on, one might expect him to eventually say, "Don't count your chickens before they hatch," or "A rolling stone gathers no moss." Luke's strange and perhaps futile effort to interpret this parable clearly demonstrates that, for Luke at least, this parable was highly ambiguous.

The riches within ambiguity need yet to be explored. Perhaps these riches can be illustrated by reflecting on what might have happened after Jesus told His followers a parable like the parable of the unjust steward. What could have happened is that people listening to Jesus walked away saying, "What was He talking about?" Some would offer their interpretations. Others would argue otherwise. May be little, if any, consensus would be reached.

But even if no consensus were reached, something happened! What happened—even before understanding took place—is that a community took shape around Jesus' Words. People who once did not know each other were now engaged in conversation, and they did so *because* Jesus' words were ambiguous. Had they completely understood Jesus, no conversation would have happened and no community would have been created. Jesus' words—by virtue of their ambiguity—drove people together. Other people must now be recognized because of His words. Furthermore, if these Words are the Word of God, the Church is being created here, and it is being created out of nothing just as the universe was created out of nothing by God's Word. It is simply another case of the Word of God creating a space for itself. Ambiguity is a prerequisite for community. We must not forget this. If ambiguity does not exist, there is no purpose in anyone's talking to anyone else. Why should we bother with such conversation? If everything is clear, we need not converse. It is because things are ambiguous that I am directed to you in conversation and in community. Ambiguity is the source of such community, and the type of community ambiguity promotes is a community of conversation.

That this community of believers may well be called a community of conversation is indicated by Matthew 18:15-20, where Matthew discusses the topic of excommunication.

> If your brother (or sister) sins against you, go and tell him his fault, between you and him alone. If he *listens* to you, you have gained your brother. But if he

> does not *listen* take one or two others along with you, that every word may be confirmed by the evidence of two or three witnesses. If he (or she) refuses to *listen* to them, tell it to the church; and if he refuses to *listen* even to the church, let him be to you as a Gentile . . . .

It is worth noting that the offense that leads to the brother being put out of the church is neither the initial sin, nor false doctrine. It is his refusal to listen? This is clearly in accord with the community of conversation around God's Word that is the prerequisite for the establishment of the Church. Conversation is quite impossible if there is no listening, consequently, not listening places one outside such a community.

This notion of a community of conversation also prefigures the type of power that is characteristic of communities that take pleasure in ambiguity. Since the Church is one such community, this notion of power prefigures the notion of power and authority that ought to be characteristic of the Church. One way to understand the nature of this power and authority is to distinguish between conversation and communication. Not all conversation is communication. A conversation might occur and no communication take place at all. Likewise, not all communication is conversation. Advertisements on television, or a memos telling a subordinate what to do, certainly communicate, but they are not conversations.

Communication that is not conversation exhibit what some people call unilateral power. The one who exercises unilateral power moves others without being moved. This is the type of power that is often employed by organizations that insist on creating the illusion that everything is clear, definite, and settled. The typical form of communication in such a setting is an office memo: the one writing the memo is immune from the one(s) to whom the memo is written. Such is typical of the employment of unilateral power.

Communication that is conversation is different. It employs another type of power called "communal" power.[14] Those who exercise communal power are influenced by others. Conversations are examples of such power because people engaged in conversation are never the same after the conversation. Conversation presupposes the capacity of those engaged to undergo change at the same time as they seek to influence and change others. Herein rests another benefit implicit in ambiguity. The conversation that ambiguity necessitates implies a type of power more consistent with the power Jesus employs because Jesus was subject to the influence of others even though He need not have been; moreover, Jesus died because He subjected Himself to the influence of others. In other words, the type of power implicit in ambiguity leads to a discussion of another benefit of ambiguity, namely, grace.

To understand the relationship between ambiguity and grace, we must back up a little and remember that one of the sources of ambiguity is the fact that Jesus is present in a medium of one kind or another. Since Jesus is not the medium, but is present within the medium, discernment is one of the activities Christians must perform when we go to places Jesus has promised to be present, and the possibility of our being able to accurately discern depends upon the bodily presence of Jesus in His medium of choice. In other words, when we discern Jesus' presence, we discern Jesus' body.[15] The question why Jesus presents Himself in a mediated, embodied way is quite significant. The answer is simple. Grace always takes an embodied, mediated form, and grace cannot assume an unmediated, disembodied state.[16]

Needless to say, this answer is easier to state than it is to argue, but argue it we must. The argument begins with a technical definition of grace. Grace is loving treatment in discontinuity with one's past. Less technically, grace means not being treated by "the book." Both definitions say the same thing. If one is treated by "the book," one is being treated in continuity with one's past. "The book" lists certain requirements, and these must be met in terms of one's past. Grace throws the book away. It treats the person in discontinuity with the past, because it grants what is needed despite what regulations might say. Matthew 20:1-15 demonstrates how grace often comes into conflict with rules and other assumptions concerning proper behavior.

> For the kingdom of heaven is like a householder who went out early in the morning to hire laborers for his vineyard. After agreeing with the laborers for a denarius a day, he sent them into his vineyard. And going out about the third hour he saw others standing idle in the market place; and to them he said, "You go into the vineyard too, and whatever is right I will give you." So they went. Going out again about the sixth hour and the ninth hour he did the same. And about the eleventh hour he went out and found others standing and he said, "Why do you stand here idle all day?" They said to him, "Because no one has hired us." He said to them, "You go into the vineyard too." And when evening came, the owner of the vineyard said to his steward, "Call the laborers and pay them their wages, beginning with last up to the first." And when those hired about the eleventh hour came, each of them received a denarius. Now when the first came, they thought they would receive more; but each of them also received a denarius. And on receiving it they grumbled at the householder saying, "These last worked only one hour, and you have made them equal to us who have born the burden of the day and the scorching heat." But he

> replied to one of them, "Friend, I have done you no wrong; did you not agree with me for a denarius? Take what belongs to you and go; I choose to give to this last as I give to you. Am I not allowed to do what I choose with what belongs to me? Or do you begrudge my generosity?"

Several things are not done "by the book" in this particular passage. The most obvious is that people are not receiving equal wages for equal work. Less obvious is the strange way the householder pays his laborers. If he had decided to violate the rule "equal pay for equal work," the smart thing to do would have been to pay the ones who worked longest first and send them home. Only after those who had worked all day were gone, should he have paid those who had not worked as long. This makes sense from an administrative point of view because it would have cut down on the public outcry. The householder, however, does not treat anyone by "the book" in this passage.

Once it is recognized that a denarius was what an average family *needed* to make it through the day, it becomes apparent why the householder refused to treat his laborers by "the book." In this case there is a conflict between treating a person lovingly and treating a person in accord with regulations. The householder chooses to give what is needed instead of what is required.

Matthew 20:1-15 also demonstrates that for the householder to treat his laborers lovingly instead of by "the book," he must also treat most of his laborers in discontinuity with their past. It was impossible for the householder to treat most of his laborers in continuity with their past and still give them what was needed. The past of most of his laborers dictated that they would receive from as little as one twelfth to as much as three quarters of what was needed.

The householder did not treat many in continuity with their past. He chose instead to give them what was needed.

This parable shows that if grace is loving treatment in discontinuity with one's past, then grace cannot be regulated. There can be no program for the administration of grace. Grace cannot be made into a book of rules because it is the very act of not being treated by a book. Rather than rules and regulations, grace depends on the presence of some*body* with the power to dispense with both regulations and propriety. That is to say, grace always takes an embodied form. In the case of the parable of the Laborers in the Vineyard, no*body* but the householder or his agent could be gracious. Grace requires the presence of some*body* who is empowered to dispense with rules.

The person who taught me that grace depends on the presence of some*body* with the power to dispense with regulations and give what is needed was a woman whom I encountered as a consequence of my parish ministry. She is not the type of person people like me might approach for insight into life's mysteries. She is one of the poor and marginalized. She is not exactly mentally retarded, but she can hardly be classified as intelligent. I have often said that she is just smart enough to have the profound emotional problems that she possesses. The way she experienced her problems compounded them and serves to illustrate her intuitive understanding of grace. According to her account, her husband had been disabled at work and was receiving social security disability payments that she believed were augmented considerably because he was married to her. Her husband left her, taking with him his social security payments. She had absolutely no source of income. She tried to go on public assistance but was told that she could not receive assistance because her husband had a good income. She refused to get a divorce because she believed that divorce was a violation of

God's eternal law. In other words, if she continued to be treated by "the book," at least as she perceived "the book," she would be left without any means of support. Her intellectual and emotional state clearly prevented her from working, and she did not fit any governmental regulation. Nevertheless, she survived. She survived because she knew that her life depended on her finding some*body* who had the power to dispense with regulations and not treat her by the book. She went to the yellow pages, and starting at the top of the list of clergy, she called each of us until she got what was needed each month. One person would provide the rent. Another provided heat. Another purchased her food. She survived. She found some*body*. After awhile, she also found somebody who could help her with government regulations, but for about two years her survival depended on the presence of some*body* with the power to dispense with regulations and treat her lovingly and in discontinuity with her past. In the process she gave more to us than we did to her, because she taught many of us about the nature of grace.

The points that I have made about grace are quite consistent with a Christian understanding of salvation. For example, the idea that grace means not being treated by the book might be translated into Paul's contention that according to the book—the Torah—we cannot possibly attain our salvation. Since the Law both tells us what is required to earn our salvation and informs us that we cannot do what is required, the Law, at least according to Paul, makes our situation quite comparable to the situation of the woman who taught me about grace. Just as there was no hope for my teacher's survival apart from her finding some*body* with the power to dispense with rules and not treat her by the book, there is no hope for us if the Law is the only means to salvation. On the basis of the Law, we merit only death or damnation. The idea that grace requires the presence of some*body* with the power to dispense with rules and act lovingly towards us corresponds to the related Pauline notion that the only hope humanity has when confronted with the impossible demands of the Law is to find some*body* with the power to dispense with the Law and give us what is needed. The good news is this *body* has found us! It is Jesus the Christ. In the end, the contention that grace is loving treatment in discontinuity with our past is derived from this notion of salvation. By encountering with Jesus, we are loved; we are given what is needed, namely, life. Such a gift demonstrates that we are treated in discontinuity with our past because, according to the Law, if we are treated in continuity with our past we merit death.

Ambiguity is the by-product of the Church happening, whenever believers gather where Jesus has promised to be. In contrast to what we sometimes feel, ambiguity has some very positive features. It creates a community based on conversation, and such a community implies a communal rather than a unilateral understanding of power. Likewise, ambiguity is a consequence of the bodily presence of Jesus within those media in which He has promised to be present. As such, ambiguity may also be a property of grace, a grace whose character becomes manifest when Jesus is discerned within the medium in which the incarnate Word has promised to be present.

This brings us once again to the need for discernment within the Church. If the presence of Jesus within the Church is ambiguous, as has been argued, it would be quite gracious indeed if the Church had a ministry concerned with discernment. It would even be better if God had established such a ministry—at least by making certain promises concerning that ministry. Something like this will be argued in the next chapter which has the ordained ministry as its principal topic.

Chapter Two

The Task and Charism of the Ordained Ministry

The ordained ministry exists because discernment is necessary to the life of the Church. It is not that the ordained are the only believers capable of discernment. Indeed, some ordained do not discern Jesus' presence very well. Rather, the tasks that the ordained perform create arenas in which discernment occurs. Discernment is not the exclusive domain of the ordained. The ordained are to make sure discernment happens, and they do so by performing the tasks that are normally associated with the ordained ministry. In other words, preaching, teaching, liturgy, evangelism, etc., actually clear arenas in which the Church can discern the presence of Jesus in media He has promised to be present. The ordained normally preside over such tasks, but the task of discerning Jesus in the media that constitute the Church remains a public, corporate event.

Because such discernment is a corporate event, the ordained seldom need to make discernments in isolation. The ordained operate with a decided handicap if they understand their task to be to discerning Jesus, in private, and then to emerge from their seclusion with answers, like the High Priest might have emerged for the Holy of Holies. It is the Body of Christ that does the discerning. The ordained try to make discernment as corporate as possible, because it is important that all of the spiritual gifts present in the Body of Christ are brought to bear on this important task.

Since true discernment happens by virtue of the gift of wisdom, it is important not to confuse wisdom with the charism bestowed at ordination. All one need do to avoid such an error is to name five ordained persons at random. Surely it will be obvious that at least one person on the list does not possess the gift of wisdom. This being said, however, it is also clear that the charism bestowed at ordination is related to wisdom because it involves establishing an arena in which wisdom and other gifts of the Spirit can be brought to bear on the tasks of discernment.

THE ORDAINED AND THE TASK OF DISCERNMENT

At first glance, it may appear too simplistic to associate creating an arena in which discernment may occur with the variety of tasks the ordained actually perform. The ordained tend to worship. They teach. They preach. They at least help in the day to day administration of the congregation. They tend to the spiritual, emotional, and physical health of the people under their care. They are called to lead lives that are above reproach. Indeed, these tasks are quite diverse, but the one thing all tasks have in common is that each helps to create an arena in which discernment can happen in the Church.

Since Jesus has made some rather specific promises concerning His presence in media that are often constitutive of worship, the ordained have always been intimately involved in worship. Since Jesus is *not* the media in which He has promised to be present, but is only present within those media, one important component of worship is the effort to make Jesus' presence in these media as unambiguous as possible. It is clear that, in the final analysis, the purpose of worship is worship! Nevertheless, the discernment of whom we are worshipping, and where the one we worship is located, is an important ingredient in the preparation for worship.

The worship of Jesus could be hampered by hymns to a goddess of fertility because such a hymn would not properly recognize the One we worship. Likewise, our worship might be hampered by the way we position ourselves when we worship. For example, a congregation that fails to minister to its community might be better served liturgically if its worshippers turned around to face the door when they worship, because Jesus may well be going out the door of the church and into the community. Proper discernment may require changes in our hymns to reduce unnecessary ambiguity. It may also require a change in our ritual. In any case, the need for discernment explains why our worship services are more often planned than they are spontaneous. They are planned to make Jesus' presence as unambiguous as possible. In worship, Jesus' presence should be as clear as we can make it in order to reduce the unnecessary ambiguities that *we* impose on the situation. We can do nothing about the ambiguities that are the consequence of the media in which Jesus has promised to be present, but we can do something about the lack of clarity that we impose. In structuring worship with the task of discernment in mind, a better witness to Jesus' presence is possible. Such a witness makes the task of ministry in every day life more likely, because it better equips believers to recognize Jesus when He is encountered where He has not promised to be, to testify to that presence, and to follow Jesus as He leads His disciples into the world.

Interestingly enough, the fact that the ordained have always been intimately involved in worship has contributed to the ambiguities that *we* impose on worship. Too often we have equated the fact of an ordained person's intimate involvement in worship with the idea that worship is the exclusive domain of the ordained. Recent efforts to involve the whole people of God in our worship services as lectors, cantors, and assistants have implicitly recognized that if worship is the exclusive domain of the ordained, ambiguities of our own design creep into our understanding of worship. As long as we equate the fact that the ordained have been intimately involved in worship with the idea that worship is the exclusive domain of the ordained, we place too much emphasis on the person of the ordained and too little on the God we worship.

In an effort to make our worship as unambiguous as possible, we must direct attention away from the ordained without, at the same time, undermining their intimate association with worship. Lay persons should preach at least enough to demonstrate that the ordained are not the only ones capable of preaching. To maintain their close association with worship, however, the ordained should help identify those people who have the gift of preaching. It is not that *anyone* should preach. It is that those with the gift of preaching should be allowed to practice their gift.

In an effort to reduce unnecessary ambiguities in worship, lay people should lead worship—indeed, lay persons should preside at the Lord's Supper—at least enough to counter the impression that the ordained are more holy than others. Again, this is not to say that we should not be concerned about who presides. As in preaching, the community must discern those who have such gifts. All that is being noted here is that our practices often transmit messages that make what we wish to proclaim far less understandable than necessary.

Our current practice of allowing only the ordained to preside at the Eucharist may teach what we do not wish to convey, as is often demonstrated when the possibility of having lay people preside at the Eucharist is discussed. In such conversations, we often encounter residue of the medieval doctrine of ordination which stated that ordination imposes an ontological change in the person enabling the ordained one to preside.[17] It is relatively easy to draw such a conclusion if, year after year, the only ones seen presiding at our Holy events are the ordained. The rite of ordination is not an initiation into a labor union that jealously guards the jobs of its members by refusing to allow others to do the tasks its members do. The rite of ordination is the beginning of a ministry that has no turf to defend.

All this is not to say that "anything goes" in worship. The character of our worship is always limited by the revelation of our God and the media in which our Lord has promised to be present. A friend of mine told me a story that illustrates this point. Two days after becoming a pastor in his second congregation, my friend had his first church council meeting. One of the items that came up for discussion at this particular meeting was the suggestion that the congregation replace the wine in the Lord's Supper with cranberry juice. Most of the council seemed excited about this innovative proposal!! After all, they reasoned, cranberry juice looked more like blood than the purple wine they were using, and cranberry juice was non-alcoholic. It was only when the council achieved apparent consensus on the issue that they turned to their new pastor for advice. Now the pastor did not like the proposal at all, but, as he tells it, he discerned the issue a little differently than most. He thought that his new council was testing his devotion to them. As he put it, "They wanted to see if I would love them even if they act silly." With this judgment in mind, the pastor said, with a note of irony that was lost on the church council, "It does not matter how you vote on this issue." The council voted to change to cranberry juice.

Because the pastor's judgment regarding the council's motives was correct, he never saw cranberry juice on the altar. In fact, the congregation never made the change. Nevertheless, the pastor knew what he would have done if cranberry juice had appeared. He would have simply given the benediction and dismissed the congregation before the Supper was to start. If people had asked him about it, he was prepared to say, "The table was not prepared." In his opinion, this could have led to a public discussion of the sacrament in the congregation where Jesus' commands could have been discussed, and His presence discerned. The discussion might also have shown how Christianity is at odds with any culture in which it is found. Even in a democracy, for example, we cannot vote on the media in which Jesus has promised to be present. For Jesus' presence to be assured, those who consider themselves to be His brothers and sisters must gather where He has promised to be present. In the case of Holy Communion, Jesus has promised to be present in a meal of bread and wine and not a meal of bread and cranberry juice. Incidentally, my friend still wishes that cranberry juice had been substituted. It would have been quite interesting.

This illustration demonstrates the pivotal role of worship in the task of discernment. Although worship is an end in itself, it does have implications that extend far beyond the actual liturgy. For example, it is essential to contrast Jesus with the culture in which we happen to reside. If my friend's congregation had placed cranberry juice on the altar, the discussion that would have resulted may have helped the congregation distinguish Jesus from democratic processes like voting. This would have been one case where democracy did not yield the truth because what was being voted on was a command of Jesus. If a contrast between Jesus and culture would have arisen in this context, this contrast might have demonstrated that worship has an important function in our efforts to create an arena in which discernments can take place even in everyday life. It is for reasons such as this, as well as the necessity of identifying Jesus' presence in places that Jesus has promised to be, that the ordained have been intimately associated with worship life. Worship, after all, creates an arena in which corporate discernments can be made.

Preaching also creates such an arena because preaching promotes conversation among the believers. What we have noted concerning Jesus' parables may be true of preaching. Even before a sermon is understood, it creates a community of conversation. Like Jesus' parables, sermons are ambiguous, and that very ambiguity is the source of preaching's strength and power; for it is by virtue of this ambiguity that conversation is necessary, and this need for conversation creates community. It is this power to create such a community of conversation that best illustrates the naked power of preaching.

Interestingly enough, however, we who preach are often quite uncomfortable with the very ambiguities that give preaching its power. The way sermons are normally delivered undermines, rather than promotes, the sort of conversation that preaching creates. It would take a courageous person, indeed, to stop a preacher in the middle of a sermon in order to engage in dialogue. It simply is not done! Moreover, there is seldom any formal structure established outside the liturgy to help people engage in the conversation that preaching promotes. As such, the arena for discernment that preaching creates often goes unrecognized.

Finally, the *way* preachers preach often tends to cut off conversation before it occurs, because preachers often present their sermons in such a way that the impression is created that the preacher has all the answers to the struggles of life, or that the Word of God causes the preacher no discomfort at all. A sermon need not be presented in this manner. It can be presented as being a part of an on-going struggle that the preacher is having with the Word of God. People are much more likely to relate to such struggles. If a preacher portrays himself or herself as struggling with the same issues of faith, a person engaged in a similar struggle is more likely to feel free to speak, and discernment is more likely to occur as a consequence. If this happens, preaching can also be understood to serve corporate discernment because it also creates an arena for conversation within the life of the Church.

What has just been said about preaching might also be said concerning teaching. The act of teaching requires that the teacher attempt to discern Jesus' presence in history, society, nature, Scripture, etc., and to testify to that presence so that the character of discipleship becomes more obvious. Understood in this important way, teaching involves discernment, witness, and discipleship, and is, therefore, a ministry of the Church. Teaching has another function, however, which demonstrates why it is a task associated with the ordained ministry. Like preaching, teaching creates an arena in which discernment might happen.

Contrary to the beliefs of many, the process or manner in which Christianity is taught is at least as important as the content of Christian teaching. This, of course, is *not* the same as saying that the content of Christianity is not important. It is, in fact, the content that makes a particular teaching, Christian. All that is being said here is that the content of Christianity can be undermined by the way it is presented.

Sometimes the way we teach is so opposed to the content and life of the very Christianity we teach that what we end up communicating is what is implicit in the process of teaching instead of Christianity's content. Some Lutherans in

America recognized this a few years ago when they tried to disassociate confirmation from first communion. One of their arguments used in support of this change was that Holy Communion was being understood as a reward for successful completion of confirmation rather than as a free, gracious gift from God. Hence, Holy Communion was understood as a work despite teachings to the contrary. The process of confirmation undermined what was being taught about Holy Communion. In the history of Christianity, there have been more severe instances of process undermining content. For centuries, we burned heretics in the name of a loving God! One wonders what sort of message that conveyed. In order to illustrate how teaching creates an arena in which discernment might occur, it is best to focus on how we teach rather than what we teach. Teaching styles that promote conversation among the faithful ought to be developed. Those that do not should be rejected. Our teaching styles should promote conversations. They should not bring them to an end. Attention to methods that promote such conversation is of fundamental importance to teaching, and only as we attend to such methods do we refrain from undermining the content we are attempting to convey. Attending to what happens when we teach helps us identify the arena for discernment that Christian teaching creates. Here believers can discern the presence of their Lord in places that He has promised to be present, testify to that presence and follow Jesus. It is because teaching creates such an arena that it, too, is considered to be among the tasks that we have traditionally associated with the ordained ministry.

Pastoral care is also a task that is normally assigned to the ordained, but, once again, it has never been the exclusive domain of the ordained. Indeed, the word "pastoral" in pastoral care may prevent some believers from recognizing that pastoral care is a responsibility of all Christians.

Pastoral care involves discerning the need of the person, and this involves creating an environment in which a person's true feelings can be expressed and the possible reasons for those feelings can be explored. Needless to say, most of the tools of psychotherapy and the social sciences can be employed to discern these needs, but if discerning needs were all that is involved in pastoral care, pastoral care would be the same as secular therapy. It is not. Pastoral care also includes the attempt to interpret the reality of the person's needs in a way that is faithful to the Lordship of Christ.

One way to understand the difference between pastoral care and more secular therapies is by examining the psychoanalytic notion of transference. Transference refers to the transfer of a person's emotional attachments from the parental figure to the care giver.[18] "In positive transference the patient loves the analyst and wishes to obtain love and emotional satisfaction from him (or her). In negative transference the patient views the analyst as an unfair, unloving, rejecting parental figure . . . ."[19] In either case transference is one of the keys to successful care, because successful care involves a reinterpretation of the facts of a person's life. For a variety of reasons, individuals adopt a specific understanding of their worth from their parental figures. In some instances, such an understanding leads to low self-esteem or other far more severe difficulties. Transference breaks the authority of such parental interpretations by transferring that authority to the therapist. If transference occurs, the therapist is in the position to reinterpret the person's life story without, at the same time, denying the facts of that story. It is hoped that such a reinterpretation of a person's life will not be as confining and restrictive as the one received from parental authority. This enables the person to better cope with life.

Pastoral care also uses the phenomenon of transference, but it is hoped that this transference will be from the parental authority to Jesus' authority. In most cases, this is impossible to accomplish without repeated testimony to the Lordship of Jesus. Indeed, the persons in need of care will often try to make the pastoral counselor into the authority, but these efforts should be noticed and used by the counselor to witness to Jesus. The reason for this is quite simple: a merely human authority can only help reinterpret the life story of a person in need. At best, this reinterpretation is less restrictive and "healthier," but even the best reinterpretation is restrictive in some sense because it still subjects the person in need to certain necessities.

People often define and order life in terms of a necessity. A necessity is different from a determination because a particular necessity need not be the only way a person orders his or her life, but it usually seems to the person in question that there are no alternatives. Perhaps a person has low self-esteem. It has neither been determined in advance that this person have low self-esteem, nor is it determined in advance that the person will always have low self-esteem. Without some kind of counseling, however, it is likely that the person will always have a low self-esteem; hence, low self-esteem is a necessity in such a case. It need not have been the case that the person in question has low-self esteem, and it need not be the case that this situation continue, but the person with low self-esteem certainly does not feel this way.

Through transference, a counselor becomes the substitute parental authority in the life of the person in need. This authority allows the counselor to reinterpret the facts of the person's life in such a way that low self-esteem is avoided. As has been said, the difference between a pastoral counselor and a secular counselor is that in secular counseling transference is made to the counselor while, in pastoral counseling, the effort is made to make the transference to Jesus and allow Jesus to reinterpret the person's life. It is as if the person in need is in a house that is too small and restrictive. The secular therapist may add a few rooms, allowing the person to move about more freely. Successful therapy provides much more room, but the person is still confined indoors. It may well be a mansion instead of a shed, and the person may never notice that he or she is still indoors, but it is still confinement. If, however, transference has been made to Jesus rather than to the therapist, the person need no longer be subject to the necessities imposed by his or her past. To use our analogy once again, one is no longer confined to the house! One is no longer subject to the constraints of indoor living!! This can happen because Jesus not only reinterprets the life of the one in need as any good therapist might, but Jesus makes the past of those in need His own. Our past no longer is the source of life's necessities. They do not define life. It is true that the past happened, but we are redeemed from the necessities of our past. Newness is a possibility because our past has been assumed by Jesus.

To even begin to express this to those under our care, an arena must be created in which Jesus' presence in the life of the person(s) in need might be discerned and a witness to that presence may be made. It has already been noted that discernment depends on knowledge of the person's life story and recognition of feelings that the person has expressed.

Pastoral care may be different in structure from other tasks associated with the ordained, because Jesus may not have been present in the life of the one under care. The fact is that Jesus has not promised to be with everyone. No specific person is a medium in which Jesus has promised to be present. This does not, however, prevent us from directing people in need of care to places where Jesus has promised to be. It is obviously appropriate to invite them to worship and to other places that Jesus has promised to be present.

It should be equally obvious that the presence of Jesus within the context of pastoral care should also be testified to if the care giver wants to promote the mystery of transference to Jesus. In any case pastoral care is impossible without discernment and witness. It relies on an arena in which discernment can occur, and it involves discerning the reality of a person's life and witnessing to the activity of Jesus in that life. When appropriate, it involves directing the person in need to places where Jesus has promised to be in the hope that His presence may heal.

Church administration has also been a task normally assigned to the ordained because Church administration is closely related to discernment. Proper church administration is nothing less than the discernment of Jesus' Spirit, which happens to be the Holy Spirit. Consequently, church administration must establish an arena where corporate discernment is possible. The administration of *any* organization depends upon the establishment and implementation of the organization's priorities, and an organization's priorities largely depend upon that organization's vision of the future. As far as the Church is concerned, the Holy Spirit is in control of the future. In the early Church, Church leaders postulated that the future was the Holy Spirit's domain stating that all activities of God originate with the Father, are presented by the Son, and are brought to perfection by the Holy Spirit.[20] Discerning the Spirit, therefore, is the same as discerning God's future. Since church administration involves discerning the future of a particular congregation, and since any church's future is God's future, it follows that church administration is synonymous with discerning the Holy Spirit. Policies and priorities ought to be established that are consistent with this future, and our implementation of these policies should not use measures that are inconsistent with this future of God. All our committees should keep this as their primary objective because the goal of administration is to discern Jesus' Spirit, to testify to it, and to act accordingly.

Finally, the ordained are called to nurture the faith of "the little ones," therefore, their public lives should be above reproach. Even though a proper public life applies to all Christians, the fact is that the behavior of the ordained often does more to undermine the faith of others than does the behavior of the laity. In I Corinthians 10:19-23, Paul acknowledges the fact that our behavior can unnecessarily obscure the Gospel, when he resolves to make himself all things to all people for the sake of the Gospel. Note, Paul does not want to make himself all things to all people. He is not advocating that one should do or say anything to gain the approval of others. He resolves to make himself all things to all people for the sake of the *Gospel.* He vows to refrain from doing things with his life that undermine his testimony to Christ. In the case of this letter to the Corinthians, Paul appears to be referring to eating meat sacrificed to idols. On the one hand, Paul acknowledges that he is free to eat such meat. On the other hand, he recognizes that eating such meat might undermine the faith of the weak. It is for their sake that Paul suggests that the Corinthians refuse meat offered to idols. Here Paul recognizes that the public behavior of Christians can lead to unnecessary confusion regarding God's Word, and that such unnecessary confusion might undermine discernment among the faithful.

Perhaps it is in this context that the relationship between ordination and issues that currently trouble us regarding who to ordain ought to be addressed. The establishment of such standards currently involves the issue of the ordination of men and women who publicly declare that they are homosexuals and vow to continue to practice homosexuality in some way. Let me be as clear as possible. The issue is not the ordination of homosexuals as such. Homosexuals have been ordained and will be ordained until the kingdom comes. The issue that faces the Church today is the ordination of men and women who *publicly declare* their practice of homosexuality. A distinction should also be made between the public declaration of one's homosexuality and privately informing some people of it. Like all people, homosexuals should have the opportunity to receive spiritual and pastoral care as they honestly struggle with their faith in the context of their lives. They too must be able to seek guidance. This is why the distinction is made between a public declaration of one's homosexuality and disclosing it to a chosen circle of fellow Christians. A public declaration informs the entire Church. It therefore includes informing those whose faith might be undermined by such a disclosure. The question therefore becomes, "Does the public disclosure of homosexuality by an ordained person seriously undermine the Church's witness in this day and age?" Another way of putting this is, "Should homosexual pastors refuse to publicly disclose their homosexuality out of their concern for those whose faith is not mature?" These questions are obviously debatable, and depend on how one interprets them in terms of Paul's vow to be all things to all people for the sake of the Gospel. Is it for the sake of the Gospel, or for the sake of something else, that an ordained person publicly discloses his or her practice of homosexuality? Much needs to be explored concerning the issue so stated, and the Body of Christ should try to discern God's will for this time and place recognizing that our conclusions need not be bound by the past or bind future generations. They must, however, be faithful to the Gospel.

To summarize, the ordained attend to worship because worship creates an arena in which Jesus can be distinguished from other candidates for deity which the world proffers. The ordained preach because the practice of preaching creates an arena of conversation around God's Word. The ordained teach because the process of teaching can establish arenas conducive to the corporate discernment of Jesus. The ordained must conduct to their personal lives to minimalize unnecessary ambiguities by seeing to it that their lives do not undermine the faith of the "little ones." The charism ordination bestows can be practiced when these tasks are practiced, but these tasks are not the charism. It is the contention of this presentation that the ordained preach, teach, and lead worship, in order to practice the separate gift that ordination itself bestows. It is to the character of this unidentified charism that we now turn.

ORDINATION AS CHARISM

In suggesting that a charism or spiritual gift is bestowed in ordination, we are differing from Christians who think that nothing special happens in the rite of ordination. It was probably in reaction to the medieval Christian teaching that ordination actually changes the ontological status of the one ordained (or makes the one ordained into an entirely new being capable of consecrating the sacraments), that many Protestant Christians came to believe that the rite of ordination is merely the public acknowledgment of the abilities and talents already possessed by the newly ordained. While it is clear that this task-oriented understanding of ordination was designed to eliminate many abuses, it is equally clear that neither the medieval Christian understanding of ordination, nor this more recent Protestant understanding, are consistent with the pastoral epistle's contention that ordination bestows a spiritual gift (*charisma*).

The task-oriented approach is inconsistent because it rejects the notion that something happens in ordination; and the medieval Christian view is problematic because it does not recognize that the bestowal of a charism differs from an ontological change. The author of I Timothy is promoting a different understanding of ordination when he writes:

> Command and teach these things. Let no one despise your youth, but set the believers an example in speech and conduct, in love, in faith, in purity. Till I come, attend to the public reading of Scripture, to preaching, to teaching. Do not neglect the gift (*charis*) you have which was given you by prophetic utterance when the council of elders laid their hands upon you. Practice these duties, devote yourself to them, so that all may see your progress. Take heed to yourself and to your teaching; hold to that, for by so doing you will save both yourself and your hearers.[21]

According to this passage, the author of I Timothy thought that the laying on of hands by the presbyters bestows a spiritual gift of some kind. Moreover, this charism can be practiced by setting an example, publicly reading Scripture (leading worship), preaching and teaching. As we have seen, these are the main tasks traditionally associated with the ordained ministry, which create an arena in which corporate discernment can happen. This close association may be reflected in I Timothy's contention that the practice of these tasks will "... save both yourself and your hearers." Finally, it appears that the charism ordination bestows is operative only in contexts created by the performance of these tasks. Herein rests the fundamental difference between understanding the rite of ordination as bestowing a charism and the medieval Christian understanding that ordination causes an ontological change. If ordination is understood as an ontological change, then it does not matter what the ordained do after ordination. They will still be a substantially different person and probably should be treated accordingly. If, on the other hand, ordination bestows a charism, the gift only becomes operative when it is used, and it can only be used in contexts created by the practice of tasks normally done by the ordained. If the gift is not used, it does nothing to build up the Body. Moreover, understanding ordination as bestowing a charism excludes us from saying that an ontological change has taken place, because the bestowal of a charism is not the same as an ontological change. A person with the gift of healing is still the same person. A person who has been ordained is still the same person. They may have different spiritual gifts, but there has been no ontological change. If ordination bestows a charism, it bestows a power. If the power is not exercised, it is *as if* no gift had been bestowed. Ordination bestows no power on those who do not use their gift. This may explain a great deal about some of the ordained who do not appear to be gifted at all. They simply do not use their gift. They are like the healer who does not heal. It is *as if* no gift had been bestowed because the gift is not being employed.

The fact that a gift is bestowed by the rite of ordination, and the fact that the gift can be used, do not bring us much closer to understanding ordination's character, however. The only thing that is stated in I Timothy 4:11-16 is that the practice of this charism will save both Timothy and his hearers.[22] The explicit character of this charism is not delineated. The following is an effort to speculate on its character given some of the things that have been discussed to this point.

It has been stated that the charism received through ordination is bestowed through a medium, namely, the "laying on of hands." According to I Timothy 4:14, the charism is bestowed by the presbyters who lay on hands, and in II Timothy 1:6 direct continuity with the Apostle Paul is implied by the text when the author writes in Paul's name, "Therefore, I remind you: rekindle the gift of God (*charism tou theou*) which is in you through the laying on of *my* hands." While the participation of the presbyters in ordination is not explicitly excluded in this verse,[23] in this passage we have a clear illustration of the importance of apostolic continuity. This emphasis is probably due to the special authority of the apostles present very early in the Church. We see such an emphasis in the Apostolic Commission of Matthew 28:17-20.

> And Jesus said to them, "All authority in heaven and on earth has been given to me. Go, therefore, and make disciples of all nations, baptizing them in the name of the Father and of the Son and of the Holy Spirit, teaching them to observe all that I have commanded you, and lo, I am with you always, to the close of the age."

For many good reasons, it is often deemed inappropriate to compare passages from one book in the New Testament with another. The Bible, after all, is more like a library than a single book, consequently, a passage from one book in this library might have little to do with a passage from another. Nevertheless, there are several good reasons to do the unorthodox and to compare the Apostolic Commission with texts in the pastoral epistles that have to do with ordination.

First, the tradition has—rightly or wrongly—described ordination in terms of apostolic continuity. The authority of the ordained has always had something to do with the authority of the apostles; thus, the traditional association between apostolic authority and ordination has something to contribute to the character of the charism that ordination bestows. Second, there are some remarkable similarities between the Apostolic Commission and the ordination rite that the Pastorals present. I Timothy 4:11-16 ascribes certain tasks to the ordained, and the practice of these tasks actually creates the context in which the charism bestowed at ordination operates. This is so important to an understanding of the character of the charism ordination bestows that it bears repeating. The tasks that have been traditionally associated with the ordained ministry have been associated with the ordained ministry because they create the context in which the charism ordination bestows can operate. All charisma require certain contexts, and the charism ordination bestows is no exception. Whereas healing requires the context of disease, and interpretation of tongues requires the context of confusion, ordination requires the creation of an arena for discernment. Moreover, this arena is created by the very tasks we normally ascribe to the ordained! Do not be confused by the fact that most of these tasks are themselves charisms. What is being said here is that charisms like preaching and teaching create arenas in which the charism bestowed in ordination operates. Ordination bestows an unnamed charism that services many other spiritual gifts.

The relationship between the understanding of ordination present in the Pastoral Epistles and the Apostolic Commission that Matthew presents is that both establish some of the tasks of the ordained and apostolic ministry. The Pastoral Epistles indicate that some tasks are preaching, teaching, care of one's public life and leading worship. The Apostolic Commission recognizes that the tasks are also evangelism, baptizing in the Triune name, and teaching all

Jesus has commanded. In both instances, the performance of these tasks create arenas in which the unnamed charism that ordination bestows can operate. Thus, in the Pastorals, the ordained are challenged to do certain tasks which create the context in which their charism will be operative. In the Apostolic Commission, the disciples are commanded to do certain tasks, which also become the context in which the power and authority that Jesus confers on them becomes operative. This is why the tasks of evangelism, preaching, teaching, leading worship baptizing, etc., have always been closely associated with the ordained. The charism bestowed in ordination is the presence and power of Jesus whenever the ordained are present in arenas in which discernment occurs, and these arenas are created by the performance of these tasks.

The fact that the charism ordination bestows and the Apostolic Commission are similar in structure does not mean that there is a clear relationship between the *charisma tou theou* (gift of the Spirit) bestowed at ordination and the Apostolic Commission. While this relationship cannot be worked out with absolute certainty, the consideration of certain facts might be helpful. Of importance is the fact that Matthew never uses the word *charisma*.[24] This means that if Matthew wished to convey something similar to what the phrase *charisma tou theou* conveys, he employed another word. To test this hypothesis, however, it is necessary to discuss certain aspects of Paul's notion of *charisma tou theou,* and to assume that the pastoral epistles are written in Paul's spirit. The Pauline word *charisma* is closely related to the word *charis* which is the word we often translate as grace. Unlike those who used *charis* to express the nature of God, Paul often used the word to express the structure of the salvation event.[25] *Charis* is something that happened. Only in a secondary sense does *charis* reveal a divine attribute.

Charis happened in Jesus' life, death and resurrection. *Charis* happened to Paul when be became an apostle. *Charis* happened most completely on the cross. Since all these events happened in history, it is said that Paul's understanding of *charis* presupposes the fundamental importance of Jesus' presence among us.[26] If the use of the word *charis* in the pastoral epistles is similar to the Pauline usage, then the grace that is bestowed at ordination refers to that which "happens" in ordination. Where the author of I Timothy warns Timothy not to "neglect the gift (*charis*) you have, which was given you by prophetic utterance when the council of elders laid their hands upon you," the author was talking about an historical event which had a particular structure. This was an event in which a grace or charism was bestowed. Grace had happened to the ordinand because of God's presence and power.[27]

In addition to its association with *charis, charisma* is also associated with the word *pneuma* (spirit) in Pauline writings. As such *charisma* refers to the saving presence just described, coupled with the power present in the saving act.[28] Thus, the presence that is associated with the word *charisma* does not refer to some unspecified being there. It is a presence with power. It is a presence with the power that God bestows, and God bestows the power of life!!! All *charisma* are Jesus' presence plus His life giving power, and the ordained can rely on this presence and power whenever they use their gift. Since the charism that ordination bestows is not specifically named, except to say that its practice means salvation for ". . . yourself and your hearers," here too we might emphasize our major contention about ordination, namely, that the tasks we normally associate with the ordained constitute the context in which the charism ordination bestows is exercised.

If this is the case, there is some similarity between the Pauline use of *charisma* and that which is being discussed in the Apostolic Commission. The Apostolic Commission begins with the familiar phrase, "All authority (*exousia*) in heaven and on earth has been given to me." Here the word authority is a translation of the word *exousia* instead of a word like *dunamis* (power). This is significant because *exousia* does not refer to an indwelling, objective, physical power that is inherent in the individual, as the word *dunamis* might. *Exousia* refers to a power that is given to an individual from an external source. This is neither mere authority nor mere power. It is a combination of both power and authority. This is an important distinction to make because it is quite possible to have the authority to do something and lack the power to do it. A police officer may well have the authority to arrest a drug dealer, but, for a variety of reasons, the police officer might lack the power to do so. The drug dealer may have political connections, or physically be able to prevent the arrest. In such cases the authority to arrest might be present without the power to do so. By the same token, it is quite possible to have the power to do something and lack the authority to do it. A fourteen year old girl might have the power and ability to drive a car, but lack the necessary authority, namely, a driver's license.

There is a difference between power and authority. The presence of one does not guarantee the presence of the other. *Exousia* is a word that combines both power and authority. When Jesus says, "All authority (*exousia*) in heaven and on earth has been given me . . . " He is claiming nothing less than what has been claimed throughout Matthew's Gospel. He is claiming that He does not just possess the internal power to forgive sins, to teach and to cast out demons. He is claiming He has the external, God-given authority to do so as well.[29] More important for this story, however, is the fact that the *exousia* of Jesus is now the same as the *exousia* of the apostles.[30] Because of Jesus' presence, and because all *exousia* has been given Jesus, the apostles have the power and authority to act and teach in Jesus name, and, at least according to the tradition, they have the authority and power to bestow this *exousia* on others. In any case, it is quite possible that the presence and power that constitute the charism bestowed in ordination, also constitute the apostolic commission. Moreover, in both cases, Jesus' presence and His power are associated with the practice of tasks ascribed to the ordained ministry.

If this interpretation is correct, the gift bestowed at ordination is *not* the ability to accurately discern Jesus in the midst of those media in which He has promised to be present. The charism of ordination is no more or less than Jesus' promise of His presence and life giving power which becomes operative whenever an ordained person is present in an arena created for discerning Jesus' presence. In other words, the tasks normally associated with the ordained ministry create arenas for the discernment of Jesus' presence. The ordained are called to perform these tasks because it is very likely that they will be present in these arenas if they perform them. Their presence in such arenas guarantees that Jesus' presence and power (the definition of a charism) will be operative, and this presence and power is God's activity of life in a context that can be confusing and divisive; for, trying to discern Jesus presence within the media in which He presents Himself may not be community building under all circumstances. It is difficult and threatening work, but it is work that is essential to intentional ministry. At the very center of ministry—the area of discernment—there is a charism bestowed by the Church on the ordained. This charism supports the Church's ministry at its very core because it is a charism that operates in the often divisive context of discernment. In this way, it might be said that the charism bestowed upon ordination guarantees the Church's unity if it is used.

There are a number of important things we now need to note. In the first place, this theory allows us to understand the office of the ordained ministry as God's gracious gift to the Church. We have seen that Jesus' presence is always ambiguous. We have argued that the task of the community of believers is to discern Jesus' presence despite this ambiguity and to testify to that presence, even though there is no guarantee that our discernment will be accurate. What is guaranteed in the charism that ordination bestows is Jesus' presence even in the midst of the errors that are sure to arise when the Body of Christ attempts to discern. This should not serve as a rationalization for complacency, for it must be remembered that Jesus' presence may be for the purpose of judgment as well as of grace. Salvation still depends on Jesus rather than on our discernment of Him.

Secondly, this understanding of the charism ordination bestows accounts for the fact that the non-ordained have always practiced the tasks normally associated with the ordained ministry. This understanding has stressed the importance of the ordained performing these tasks because performing these tasks places the ordained in contexts where their charism can operate, however, it is not absolutely necessary that these tasks be performed by the ordained for the ordained to be present in such contexts. The ordained can be present when someone else with the gift of preaching preaches and still be present in the arena preaching creates, and, while it is much better for the Church to have an ordained person present when the tasks that clear such arenas are performed, it is not necessary because most of the tasks that create such arenas are themselves charisms, and all charisms have an integrity of their own.

If this is true, the facts of Church history a
by this theory concerning the charism ordina
Throughout the history of the Church, the r
have done all of the tasks we usually associate with the ordained ministry. Moreover, there have usually been dire consequences whenever the ordained have attempted to make one task or another the exclusive domain of the ordained. For example, the medieval Christian understanding of ordination both established the mass as the exclusive domain of the ordained and created a situation that, for all practical purposes, often excommunicated the poor. It is well documented that the Roman Catholic mission to Latin America, for example, paid this price because there simply were not enough priests to go around. Since those with money were more likely to attract priests, the poor suffered. Because the poor were unlikely to see but few priests, they were, in effect, denied the sacraments simply because they were poor.[31] Likewise, those who still wish to make presiding at the Lord's Supper the exclusive domain of the clergy run the risk of denying the sacrament to those in smaller congregations who cannot afford a pastor. The contention that the charism ordination bestows is the presence and power of Jesus when the ordained are present in arenas of discernment created by preaching, teaching, etc., would prevent such errors because it recognizes that there is no task that is the exclusive domain of the ordained.

At the same time, this theory recognizes why these tasks are important for the ordained to do. Describing the unnamed charism ordination bestows as the life giving presence and power of Jesus given to the ordained by the Church and operative in contexts created by the very tasks often associated with the ordained ministry, actually accounts for the fact that the Church has often associated certain tasks with the ordained ministry. According to the texts from I 'imothy and Matthew, ordination's charism can be practiced in contexts created by preaching, teaching, leading worship, tending to one's life, baptizing in the Triune name and through missionary activity. The fact that the charism ordination bestows can only be practiced in contexts created by these tasks accounts for the traditional association between the ordained and these tasks. To place this discussion in the systematic context of chapter one, the ordained are involved in certain tasks because the practice of the these tasks clears an arena in which corporate discernment can happen, and it is precisely in this arena that the charism bestowed at ordination becomes operative. These specific tasks are not exclusive to the ordained. They have never been, but one reason these tasks are done by the ordained and others is so that the context necessary for the employment of the charism of ordination bestows can be created. Once again, just as the charism of healing requires disease as a context, so the charism bestowed at ordination requires the creation of an arena for discernment, and this arena is created by preaching, teaching, worship, attention to one's public life and baptizing in the name of the Triune God.

Finally, this understanding of ordination is different from two dominant views. The first is the notion that ordination bestows an ontological change on the one being ordained that changes the individual so drastically that he or she now has the super-human power to make Jesus be present in the Eucharist and other sacraments. Ordination, however, does not bestow such a fundamental change on the one ordained. It bestows a charism, and, like all spiritual gifts, the charism ordination bestows does not imply a substantial change. It does imply a change. Like the one granted the gift of healing, a change has occurred in the one ordained, but the change is not substantial. As the one gifted with healing is still a human being with a gift, so is the one ordained. The gift makes you different, but it does not make you a new creation. Only baptism does this.

This account of ordination also differs from the functional view of ordination that states that nothing happens in ordination per se because ordination merely recognizes the fact that a person can perform certain task like preaching, teaching and leading worship. While agreeing that it is important to discern whether or not a potential ordinand can perform such tasks, this understanding of ordination does not equate these functions with the ordained ministry. These functions are important because they create the context in which the charism ordination bestows is exercised. They do not, however, constitute that charism. The charism ordination bestows remains the life giving presence and power of Jesus that is embodied by the ordained in arenas of discernment which are created by the tasks normally associated with the ordained.

IN DEFENSE OF PRESENCE

Those who are schooled in the western tradition may take very little comfort in the suggestion that the charism ordination bestows is the presence and power of Jesus when the ordained participate in arenas created for corporate discernment of Jesus. No doubt, most of us would prefer this charism to be the ability to discern Jesus' presence accurately, but such a contention would simply not be true. Not only is it an improper interpretation of the texts, the ordained simply do not always discern Jesus accurately. The ordained are often at odds with each other in their efforts to discern Jesus' presence. Often their faithful attempts to discern Jesus lead to conclusions that are clearly mutually exclusive. We need a little more agreement to even entertain the belief that the charism bestowed at ordination is the ability to accurately discern Jesus' presence. The contention that this charism is the presence and power of Jesus that occurs whenever the ordained themselves are present in arenas created for the corporate discernment of Jesus is a far more accurate reflection of reality, and a better interpretation of the texts dealing with ordination.

Nevertheless, we prefer accuracy to presence. This preference may have its origin in western philosophy which maintained that accuracy and precision in discernment were far more important than presence. Western philosophy began with a question that required a precise discernment of the truth, and for many years proceeded as if this discernment would somehow settle everything. Tradition has it that a person called Thales began philosophy and the subsequent intellectual quest of the western world with the question, "Does anything persist?" He offered his generation the discernment that water persists and remains unchanged. Despite such clarity, this proposition did not please everyone because others followed with their own candidates for that which persists and remains unchanged. Some maintained that it was earth. Others said it was fire. Another said infinity, and some said Being. Still others, the intellectual predecessors of those the philosophical tradition calls the skeptics, asserted that nothing remained unchanged. In any case, what proved to be decisive was not the answers. It was the question, "Does anything persist?" The question itself was seldom challenged in the ancient world, and the process of providing clear, propositional statements as answers to questions such as this has culminated in the importance that the western world places on accurate discernment in our verbal and written responses to such questions.

Owing to this heritage, we of the western traditions often act as if accurate discernment is fundamental, and disregard the possibility that presence could be more fundamental. We should not, however, disregard this possibility. The example of what often happens at a funeral serves is illustrative. At a funeral those who mourn often ask the question, "Why did she have to die?" It is almost as if discerning the true answer to this question will somehow alleviate the pain of the loss that is being experienced, but such a response—even if it is true and accurate—would undermine ministry. After all, sometimes the reason a person dies is quite clear. There are medical reasons. There may be social or psychological reasons. There certainly are theological reasons, but a major mistake would be made if a pastor actually answered the pleas to discern the reasons for the beloved's death. It might be very accurate, but a grave error if the pastor were to say, "The wages of sin are death, and it is well known that Joan was a particularly accomplished sinner, therefore, Joan died young." It would be a grave error to say this even if this discernment is accurate! This is the case because there are some things that are more important to us than discerning accurately, and one of these is presence. The presence of the dead loved one is primarily desired, but probably impossible. The presence of a friend is important, but the presence of a God who refuses to abandon us in our suffering is an ultimate necessity. In situations such as the death of a loved one, presence is more important than answers.

Another way to examine the possibility that presence has priority over accurate discernment is to distinguish between a problem and a crisis. A problem is a difficulty that can be resolved, given the resources already possessed by the one(s) having the difficulty. In middle class America, the breakdown of a car is normally a problem because the resources needed to resolve the difficulty are available. Normally, a car can be fixed given the resources at the disposal of its operator. For most of us, an automobile mechanic and a credit card are such resources. Others employ their own tools and labor. An accurate discernment of the difficulty coupled with the resources necessary to address the problem is all that is necessary. A crisis, however, is quite different. This is a difficulty that challenges the very resources that are normally used to solve problems. Losing a spouse due to death or divorce is a crisis if the spouse functioned as a resource that helped solve problems of child rearing, money or companionship. Without that spouse a crisis exists because the very resource once used to solve problems has been withdrawn.[32]

One important difference between a problem and a crisis stems from the different manner that each is addressed. Problems are resolved by accurately discerning the resource necessary to resolve the difficulty. If this resource has been adequately discerned and implemented, the problem is quickly resolved. If someone asks a pastor, "Pastor, where do you find that passage in the Bible that says, 'For God so loved the world that He gave His only Son . . . ' " the pastor would do well to answer, "John 3:16." This would be an adequate response because it gives the resource necessary to resolve the difficulty. Crises, however, are addressed differently. They are addressed by presence. If a man says that he has A.I.D.S., he probably does not want a lecture that accurately discerns the reasons that he acquired the disease. When a man says that he has A.I.D.S., he is asking for, but is often denied, presence and love. The man is in crisis. All the resources he had normally employed to solve his difficulties are threatened. His life's savings will probably be exhausted. His friends will probably abandon him. His very body will cease to be available to him. Moreover, as long as this presence and love is denied, as long as A.I.D.S. is treated as a new form of leprosy, it is less likely that a cure will be found. If a cure is not found, A.I.D.S. will remain a crisis. What is needed in a crisis is presence. The presence and love of others is the only proper way to address this crisis.

The victims of this dreaded disease can take solace in the fact that Jesus is such an Other. This Lord does not abandon people to their suffering. This Jesus does not give the dogmatic assertions that are offered by some of His pastors and priests. He offers Himself by becoming helpless and in agony on the cross. His death and resurrection testify to the fact that this God is present in the midst of crises like the A.I.D.S. epidemic.

The fact that presence is the appropriate way to address crises is further demonstrated in the book of Job. This story begins by describing Job as "blameless and upright, one who feared God and turned away from evil." While some modern theologians might contend that a man so described could not have existed, the dominant theological interpretation operative at the time Job was written, declared that although such a man might exist, he could not suffer. The theology behind such a contention was simple: suffering is *always* a consequence of one's sin, and it can be avoided if one does not sin or if one repents of one's sins. A blameless one does not sin, therefore, a blameless one does not suffer. A repentant one does not suffer because he or she is counted sinless. In other words, this interpretation of the relationship between sin and suffering made suffering a problem rather than a crisis. Since both not sinning and repentance was a possibility, suffering could be handled with the resources at one's disposal. In Job's case the resource is repentance. Indeed, this is exactly the interpretation Job's "friends" bring to their conversation with Job. Since Eliphaz, Bildad, and Zophar continue to maintain that Job's suffering can be remedied by repentance, they cannot offer their presence to Job in the midst of his suffering. They can only offer their own "accurate discernments" of Job's situation. In understanding Job's situation as a problem rather than as the crisis it is, they offer only trite theological discernments. Accordingly, they respond inappropriately. In the end, it is only God who offers presence. This God even refuses to answer Job's questions! Instead, this God gives the presence that Job needed. Even though God's presence in this case is not all that comforting, it is an appropriate response to Job's crisis.

The importance of the charism bestowed by ordination can be recognized only if one acknowledges that humanity is fundamentally in crisis. Needless to say, the crisis in which humanity finds itself has been articulated in various ways at various times in the history of the Church. For example, in the fourth century the famous heretic Arius stated the belief that Jesus was a creature in whom we have a model of salvation. He believed that human beings can obtain salvation by repenting their sins and following the model that Jesus established.[33] That is to say, Arius believed that sin was only a problem that could be solved, given the resource of repentance. Arius' most famous opponent, St. Athanasius, understood the matter quite differently. One of the many reasons Athanasius disagreed with Arius was that Athanasius thought that the fall was much more than a simple transgression that could be remedied by repentance. He believed that the fall resulted in the degeneration of our condition. Athanasius held that humanity is under the dominion of death as well as of sin as a consequence of this degeneration. Accordingly, mere repentance cannot lead to salvation since mere repentance does not adequately address our decaying condition. Humanity has to be pulled out of this condition of decay and corruption, and this requires the presence and the power of the same God who created the world from nothing.[34] Athanasius' contention that Jesus is this God had much to do with his belief that humanity is in crisis by virtue of its bondage to death. People cannot extract themselves from this bondage because the very resources they would use to do so are themselves in bondage to death. The presence and power of one not subject to death's dominion are required for salvation. The crisis created by our condition is not adequately addressed by accurately discerning the situation. Much more is needed. According to Athanasius, this crisis is addressed only by the presence and power of Jesus, who pulls us out of our bondage to sin and death and, in so doing, makes salvation a reality.

If the human condition can be described by the word "crisis," this brief inquiry into the understanding of the human condition implicit in St. Athanasius illustrates how presence may be far more important than accurate discernment in addressing this situation. This is not to say that accurate discernment is not important, but accurate discernment is not as fundamental as presence. In response to the fact of sin, evil, and suffering in the world, God does not bestow a logically coherent theodicy. Instead of a precise philosophy, God gives us Jesus the Christ, who addresses the plight of humanity with His presence. If Jesus is Lord, His presence is far more important than any philosophy or theology about His presence no matter how accurate the discernments of such speculations might be.

Let this serve as a defense of presence and also help to illustrate the importance of the statement that the charism bestowed in ordination is the presence and power of Jesus when the ordained carry this charism into arenas where discernment of Jesus occurs. If presence is the most appropriate way to address a crisis, and if the human condition is one of crisis, such a charism is a gracious gift indeed.

THE CHARISM ORDINATION BESTOWS AND OTHER GIFTS OF THE SPIRIT

Unlike other gifts of the spirit such as healing, prophecy, and speaking in tongues, the charism ordination bestows has no name. It has been described as the presence and power of

Jesus in arenas in which corporate discernment takes place, and while a description is always more cumbersome than a name, this description enables the articulation of the similarities and differences between the charism that ordination bestows and other gifts of the spirit.

In the first place, it must be noted that all charisma have one thing in common: they are all manifestations of the presence and power of Jesus. As such, they are all manifestations of the Spirit of Jesus which we have named the Holy Spirit. In their attempt to describe God as Triune, the Cappadocian theologians of the fourth century declared that all activities of God originate in the Father, are presented by the Son, and are brought to perfection by the Holy Spirit.[35] All gifts of the Spirit, therefore, are the presence of God's future. They are all manifestations of Jesus' full power as He comes as victorious Lord. Since such power is the power of life, all gifts of the Spirit breathe life into the context in which they become manifest.

Despite their similarities, however, not all gifts of the Spirit are the same. They differ from one another by virtue of the context in which they operate. The gift of healing is the presence and power of Jesus that is manifest in the context of disease. Without a disease of some sort, there would be no healing. Likewise, the interpretation of tongues is the presence and power of Jesus that manifests itself in the very human context of the failure of our conversations to communicate. Having just returned from a conference of theologians, it is now clear to me that the gift of interpreting tongues has a far broader context than the interpretation of glossolalia. We desperately needed someone with this gift, at this conference, even though we were all speaking English. In any case, interpreting of tongues is possible only in the context of the human inability to communicate. Because it is the presence and power of Jesus, this gift grants life to these situations, and like all such gifts of the Spirit, it has its own particular context, and this charism would not operate if such contexts did not exist. If everyone understood everyone else, there would be no need to interpret our many strange tongues.

With the exception of the gifts of faith, hope and love, all gifts of the Spirit will fade away with the coming of the Kingdom.[36] They will not fade because Jesus presence will be withdrawn. They will fade because the contexts in which they operate will be no more. Faith, hope, and love will abide because they exist in the context of God's final rule. They are still dependent on a context, but their context is not eliminated by the eschaton.

In any case, the charism bestowed in ordination is like other spiritual gifts in the sense that it too is the presence and power of Jesus in a specific context. As has been argued, this context is the arenas created for the purpose of discerning Christ when the tasks we normally associate with the ordained are done. As a healer must go to a place where there is disease in order to exercise the charism of healing, so the performance of tasks normally associated with the ordained place the ordained in the position to exercise their charism.

The gifts of the Spirit are named according to our varying conceptions of them, and we have these varying conceptions because of the variety of contexts in which the Spirit of our Lord operates. Yet these gifts are quite similar in the sense that they give life to the context in which they are exercised. The one who heals may be said to give life in the context of disease, and the one who interprets tongues may be said to give life to a community in the grip of confusion. By the same token, the charism that ordination bestows gives life to the Church's ministry because it promotes discernment, and, to a lesser extent, witness and discipleship to would-be ministers by granting the courage to discern.

Because the charism bestowed on the ordained grants Jesus' presence in the context of the Church's discernment, the community's actions need not be paralyzed by fear of error or inaccuracy in discernment. If Jesus were not present from the beginning, the Church, in its fear of error, might become a mere bearer of a dead tradition rather than a living community. It is Jesus' presence that grants believers the courage to discern, to witness, and to follow their Lord; for believers know that this Lord can achieve His purposes even through our errors and sins. In this sense, the charism bestowed in ordination gives life to all the ministries of the Church because it grants the courage to begin the bold venture of ministry. Like all other charisms, the charism that ordination bestows gives life. Like all other charisms, the charism ordination bestows builds up the body. If the Church did not use this charism, its mission and ministry would be handicapped. By intentionally appropriating the charism that ordination bestows, we can begin to eliminate this handicap and build up the Body of Christ.

Finally, the charism that ordination bestows differs from other spiritual gifts in one very important way. This gift is bestowed at the discretion of the Church. The Church has no say about who will receive the gifts of healing, preaching, prophecy, tongues, or any other charism that Paul lists. The Church does have a say concerning who will receive the charism ordination bestows. It is in this way that God bestows grace upon the chosen people whose characteristic state is often steeped in ambiguity. This may well be God's way of saying to the whole people of God, "I am with you in the midst of uncertainty and despair." Perhaps this, more than anything else, points to the unifying character of the ordained ministry.

Chapter Three

Pastoral Authority

Chapter II explored the character of the spiritual gift that ordination bestows, and suggested that this charism is the presence and power of Jesus that occurs in arenas created preaching, teaching, worship, etc. Still to be considered is the second component of the charism bestowed by ordination, namely, the power and authority Jesus bestows. The two words power and authority are an effort to capture the meaning of the Greek word *exousia*. *Exousia* does not refer to an indwelling, objective, physical power inherent in an individual or group. *Exousia* refers to a power that is received from some external source. Thus, *exousia* should be translated as power and authority because the word power recognizes that the recipient of *exousia* has certain capacities, and the word authority recognizes that the recipient receives this power from another. Since Jesus has *exousia* which He gives to his apostles, an analysis of Jesus' power and authority will precede a study of the power and authority that is bestowed on Jesus' followers. In both discussions, it will be argued that Jesus' life, crucifixion, death, and resurrection demand an understanding of power and authority that is quite contrary to that which we normally take power and authority to be. Indeed, if we were to label Jesus' power and authority according to our sexual stereotypes, the power and authority Jesus bestows is far more consistent with characteristics we call feminine than it is with our so-called masculine characteristics. It is in accord with this observation that the issue of the ordination of women will be addressed.

THE POWER AND AUTHORITY OF JESUS

The cross of Christ best demonstrates the character of Jesus' power and authority. On the cross, Jesus became cursed as we are cursed. On the cross, Jesus died as we die. On the cross, Jesus became available to all humanity because, on the cross, Jesus died a slave's death. Had Jesus been a banker who died of natural causes, for example, the universality of His death would have been, at the least, questionable. There would always have been some question about His having anything to do with those without money. If the Lord of the universe had been incarnate as a banker, salvation might be available only to people with bank accounts, or at least large mortgages. What, after all, does a banker have to say to someone without money? Jesus presence among us as a peasant carpenter who died a death normally reserved for slaves, however, suggests that He is available to all people because all people have the capacity to possess nothing. The mode of Jesus' presence reveals His universality. Likewise, the mode of Jesus' presence reveals the nature of His power and authority. His power is synonymous with self-emptying. It is not to be identified with grand displays. His power is not worldly power. If Jesus is Lord, authority and power are quite different from what we normally take them to be.

One way to discuss Jesus' presence, power, and authority is to back up a little bit and explore some of what the Old Testament tells us about the presence and power of God.

Terence E. Fretheim's discussion of divine presence and power in his book *The Suffering of God* is particularly illustrative.[37] He begins by recognizing that God's presence in the created order undergirds all forms of presence. In other words, when we speak of God's presence in the structure and design of creation, we cannot say that God is absent and, at the same time, be consistent with the Old Testament. "Without this as a given . . . the idea of God who is present can be perceived only as an interpretation of the natural order, or as radically discontinuous from life in creation . . . ."[38] Systematically, this sort of divine presence may be called God's sustaining activity, and God's sustaining activity is God's way of being present to all people.

It is only on the foundation of this important notion of presence that Fretheim discusses the varying degrees of intensity of God's presence in relation to Israel. Here he makes the significant observation that while God is always present in sustaining the created order, the intensity of God's presence "is significantly affected by human experience."[39] In other words, divine presence is affected by the activity of God's chosen people. When they make the climate in which God is present incompatible with divine life, God withdraws just far enough to protect His own life.

The reason for God's withdrawal becomes apparent when it is noted that God's very life is intimately associated with His promises.[40] In other words, if the God of Abraham and Sarah does not keep His promises, there is some question about whether this God is God. This relationship between God's very being and God's promises is demonstrated again and again throughout Scripture. A very strange text that might be illustrative of this point is Genesis 15: 7-11; 17.

> And God said to Abram, "I am the Lord who brought you from Ur of the Chaldeans, to give you this land to possess." But Abram said, "O Lord God, how am I to

> know that I possess it?" He said to him, "Bring me a heifer three years old, and a she goat three years old, a turtle dove and a young pigeon." And he brought Him all these, cut them in two, and laid each half over against the other, but he did not cut the birds in two. And when birds of prey came down upon the carcasses, Abram drove them away . . . .
>
> When the sun had gone down and it was dark, behold a smoking fire pot and a flaming torch passed through these pieces. On that day the Lord made a covenant with Abram . . . .[41]

This story is strange, funny, and interesting. Moreover, it may demonstrate the relationship between God's life and God's promises. It is strange because it is pretty tough to say what is going on here. It is funny because, in answer to Abram's question, "How am I to know that I'll possess it?" (Another way to say this is, "How do I know that you're telling me the truth?"), God tells Abram to bring Him a bunch of animals. To us this hardly appears to be an answer to the question, but Abram and those who read this text probably understood what was happening when Abram brings the animals and dutifully bisects them. Finally, a "smoking fire pot and a flaming torch" passed through these bisected parts. Probably no one knows what this means, but two scholars have suggested that this ritual may actually be an answer to Abram's question, "How do I know you are telling the truth?" Foster McCurley and John Reuman suggestion that the one who passes through those bisected bodies was in fact guaranteeing promises with his or her life may help us in the interpretation of this text. If the God of Abraham and Sarah is "the flaming torch" that passed through these bisected animals, this God is guaranteeing His promises to Abraham with His life.[42] Hence, there may be a close relationship between God's promises and God's life. If God's promises are not fulfilled, God's life is in jeopardy. If God's promises are not kept, God dies. With this in mind, we can resume Fretheim's discussion of God's presence and absence in the Old Testament.

In the Old Testament, God often withdraws enough to reduce the intensity of presence. This withdrawal, however, is seldom described as a complete absence. Normally God's increased distance marks another type of presence, namely, wrath. It appears to work like this: Because of Israel's sins, God finds that His presence with Israel is incompatible with His life and promises. As a consequence, God withdraws far enough to protect both His life and His promises. The result is that Israel's enemies "flow into the 'spaces' left by the divine withdrawal," and Israel experiences God's wrath.[43] God's forced departure in the Old Testament is prompted by concern for the well-being of His promises. In an effort to keep these promises, God withdraws from the chosen people precisely because their lives are incompatible with the destiny He has in store for them. God's saving promises are at stake here! God must withdraw in order to keep His promises and save His own life.

Withdrawal is only one option available to God under the conditions created by our rebellion. Another option occurred in Jesus Christ. Whereas God's tactic in the Old Testament was to withdraw whenever the lives of the chosen people became incompatible with divine being, in Jesus Christ God insisted on being present even though the lives of God's people remained inconsistent with divine life! Thus, Jesus is the fulfillment of God's promises to Israel and to humanity. Furthermore, it is this very fulfillment that kills Jesus. The promises that are fulfilled in Jesus are fulfilled only because Jesus refuses to absent Himself from an environment that is lethal to His being. In the Old Testament, God withdrew whenever Israel's life was inconsistent with His purpose and promises. Perhaps the same type of environment existed at the time of Jesus. If so, God exercises another option: God in Jesus presents Himself in and to an environment that was in opposition to divine life. This option required God's death.

It is the particular manner of Jesus' death that reveals the depth and intensity of His presence as well as the nature of His power and authority. Insofar as He insisted on being present to sinners, Jesus had to be involved in the negation of life we call sin, but, more than even this, Jesus' presence meant that Jesus be viewed as a sinner. In commenting on Paul's letter to the Galatians, Martin Luther made exactly this point.

> Therefore, it was appropriate for Him to become a thief and, as Isaiah says (53:12), to be numbered among the thieves .... And all the prophets saw this that Christ was to become the greatest thief, murderer, adulterer, robber, desecrater, blasphemer, etc., there has ever been anywhere in the world. He is not acting in His own person now. Now He is not Son of God, born of the Virgin. But He is a sinner, who has and bears the sin of Paul the former blasphemer, persecutor, and assaulter; of Peter, who denied Christ; of David, who was an adulterer and murderer, and who caused the Gentiles to blaspheme the name of the Lord (Romans 2:24). In short, He has and bears all the sins of all people in His body—not in the sense that he has committed them but in the sense that he took these sins, committed by us, upon His own body in order to make satisfaction for them with His own blood.[44]

According to Luther, our sins are satisfied because Jesus made them his own by participating in all dimensions of life. Such an intense presence is of fundamental importance to Jesus' power and authority, and such intensity could not be achieved by just any death. It certainly could not have been achieved if Jesus had died of natural causes because—when you think about it—what we call death by natural causes is a luxury normally reserved for the elite. Mine workers do not normally die of natural causes; their lives would be longer were they not mine workers. The poor often die of causes that are better described as political rather than natural. Accordingly, the salvific implications of Jesus' death would not have been extended to those who "die before their time" if Jesus' death had been by natural causes. By the same token, the salvific dimensions of Jesus' death would not have been revealed if Jesus had died the death of a hero, because most of us are hardly heroic. Crucifixion was Jesus' chosen mode of death because crucifixion establishes solidarity with the very "least" of humanity and, just so, establishes the universal significance of Jesus' death.

How crucifixion establishes solidarity between Jesus and the "least" of humanity can be demonstrated by an analysis of both the Roman and Jewish understanding of crucifixion. Martin Hengel has noted that, according to Roman Law, crucifixion was the supreme capital punishment. It was thought to be even more severe than burning or decapitation.[45] Crimes meriting crucifixion included: deserting to the enemy, betraying secrets, inciting rebellion, practicing magic, committing murder, "nocturnal impiety," prophesying about the welfare of rulers, and serious cases of falsifying of wills.[46] Because of crucifixion's terrible nature, however, it was generally a punishment inflicted only upon members of the lower classes. Those of more noble birth could expect more "humane" executions. Indeed, crucifixion was often considered "the slaves' punishment" because of its purpose to deter slave rebellion which was often defined quite loosely, sometimes bordering on minor acts of disobedience.[47] Such interpretations of the law left the slaves relatively little protection against the whims of their masters and mistresses, as the following dialogue indicates.

> "Crucify that slave," says the wife. "But what crime worthy of death has he committed?" asks the husband. "Where are the witnesses? Who informed against him? Give him a hearing at least. No delay can be too long when a man's life is at stake." "What a fool you are! Do you call a slave a man? Do you say he has done no wrong? This is my will and my command. Take it as authority for the deed."[48]

The lives of slaves were in the hands of others. They could hardly think that they controlled their own destiny when their master or mistress could end their lives at any minute.

In His crucifixion, Jesus identified Himself with these lives. As such, He identified Himself with the common human plight, because what is true for the slave is actually true for the master. The master's life too can be terminated at any moment by forces beyond the master's control. If, in His death, Jesus identifies with all humanity through such powerlessness, Jesus' lordship must be of another order. His power and authority must be different from the power and authority of the world, for, in the final analysis, the world's power is the power to kill. On the cross, Jesus insisted on being available to all humanity. He submitted Himself to the power and authority of death, but He overcame this power. He conquered it. The sort of power and authority Jesus possesses, therefore, cannot be the same as the power that killed him.

Not only did Jesus live under Roman rule, He was also a Jew. Jewish culture also had some important views regarding crucifixion which further reveal the character of the authority and power that is implicit in Jesus' death. Deuteronomy 21:22, 23 says, "And if a man has committed a crime punishable by death and he is put to death and you hang him on a tree, his body shall not remain all night upon the tree, but you shall bury him the same day, for the hanged man is accursed before God. You shall not defile your land which the Lord your God gives you for an inheritance." The Torah itself cursed a person who died on the cross by placing such a person outside the covenant. According to the Law, therefore, not only was it impossible for Jesus to be the Messiah because of His crucifixion; He died cursed and outside the community of the covenant. This contradiction is central to Paul's theology because Paul understood Jesus to be the Messiah who did in fact, die cursed by God's Law. Paul saw quite clearly that according to the Law Jesus died outside fellowship with God and outside fellowship with the people of the covenant. Yet Paul also thought that the resurrection of Jesus vindicated this outcast's life and manner of death—the outlaw is now the Savior. The Law, which heretofore had been a way to salvation, was shown to be incapable of granting salvation.

> The same fact is touched upon in Hebrews 13:12ff. where the writer speaks of dying outside the camp of the people of the covenant. If we try to translate this statement into the world of our own ideas, the image of a criminal's death is joined by the other image of the man who dies in the state of godlessness. But the comparison is not an adequate one as long as we understand godlessness as being a description of a purely human attitude. In the ancient world temples were seen everywhere, visible abodes of divine presence. People were consequently also aware of the place which was removed from God, a place where the religious might not remain. Both Paul and the writer of

> Hebrews preach that Jesus did not only die a criminal's death but that He died this death outside the limits of consecrated ground.[49]

If the Roman understanding of crucifixion is combined with the Torah's teaching, Jesus' self-emptying not only includes emptying Himself of the form of God, but it also includes emptying Himself of every form of human decency. In His crucifixion, Jesus repudiates the things we accept as the best of humanity. He becomes both a slave and a criminal, or, to use Luther's words once more, He becomes "the greatest thief, murderer, adulterer, robber, desecrator, blasphemer, etc. there has ever been in the world."[50] In becoming these things for our sakes, Jesus demonstrates both the depth of His presence and the character of His power. Abandoning the cross would have meant the abandoning the majority of human beings, who can do little else but live with the reality of suffering and death.

Moreover, and most important for our purposes, when Jesus took up His cross, He rejected the lifestyles of those who seek to be masters and lords. In contrast to slaves and others who are subject to the "mastery" of others, masters do not recognize the reality of suffering and death. Questions of life and death normally do not function as the recognized background against which the masters operate. The background against which they operate can be better expressed by questions like, "Did I do better this year than last year?" or "How well will I achieve my goal if I do this rather than that?" The answer to these questions is normally given in terms of some external standard like money, status, physical or mental health. To the masters, death is normally denied, and when it comes, it is deemed an embarrassing exception to the norm.[51]

The slaves and the marginalized, with whom Jesus expresses solidarity on the cross, have no such luxury. They are surrounded by death and suffering. In other words, the lives of the marginalized are more realistic because their idols cannot fool them into believing that death is not real. As a result, the marginalized are in a better position to understand that the idols of this world offer a false security. The marginalized are also in a better position to understand that this world's idols derive their power and authority from death. The marginalized are also in a better position to understand that the authority and power these idols received from death is the power and authority to kill. It is the power and authority to turn living beings into objects to be manipulated and controlled. The marginalized recognize that the power and authority of life is much different from the power and authority of death. It is a power that refuses to turn living beings into non-living objects. There is sure to be a struggle if both the power of life and the power of death are present. The power of death will try to turn the living into objects, and if that means killing, so be it. The power of life, on the other hand, will refuse to kill even at the risk of its own demise. In the cross, we witness the power of life, for if Jesus is Lord, He had at His disposal legions of angels who could have fought for Him. But the power of death would have triumphed had they done so. Dying was the only way that the power of life could be victorious, but to die was also to risk defeat. The outcome of the battle was not known in advance, but it is known now. The power of life won.

If Jesus is Lord, issues of power and authority must be discussed anew. If Jesus is Lord, He tells us what power is, He tells us what authority is! Our relationships must be interpreted in terms of Jesus rather than something else. Accordingly, if we discuss the omnipotence of God, omnipotence cannot refer to God's absolute power to impose whatever He wills on creation; it refers to God's power to abandon power—to become the weakest of all—and yet to rule. Now that's power! Now that's authority! It is precisely this power and authority that Jesus bestows upon the ordained and other Christians. It is the only power and authority He has.

THE AUTHORITY AND POWER OF THE ORDAINED

The authority and power bestowed in ordination are grounded in the authority and power of the One who bestows them. Since Jesus' power is based upon self-emptying and love, the authority of the ordained is based on self-emptying and love. This belief is testified to in both the Gospel of John and in the synoptic Gospels:

> When He had washed their feet, and taken His garments and resumed His place, He said to them, "Do you know what I have done to you? You call me teacher and Lord and you are right, for so I am. If I, then, your teacher and Lord, have washed your feet, you also ought to wash one another's feet. For I have given you an example, that you should do as I have done to you. Truly, Truly, I say to you, a slave in not greater than his master; nor is he who is sent greater than he who sent him."[52]

Interpreters of this Johanine text often point out that the traditional relationships between teacher and disciple, master and servant, are being reversed in that text, however, the implications are even more radical, if John's explanation of that event is remembered. The teacher and Lord is the slave of His disciples for all time! As a consequence, the disciples of such a teacher must be slaves too, because the only way to follow a slave is to be a slave. It is only in and through such service that they exercise the authority and power of the Slave who conquered death.

A similar point is being made in Mark 10:35-45 when James and John approach Jesus and ask if He will allow them to sit at His right and left hands when He comes to the kingdom.

> But Jesus said to them, "You do not know what you are asking. Are you able to drink the cup that I drink, or be baptized with the baptism with which I am baptized?" And they said to Him, "We are able." And Jesus said to them, "The cup that I drink you will drink; and with the baptism with which I am baptized, you will be baptized; but to sit at my right hand or my left is not mine to grant, but it is for those for whom it has been prepared." And when the ten heard it, they were indignant against James and John. And Jesus called them to Him and said to them, "You know that those who are supposed to rule over the Gentiles lord it over them, and their great men exercise authority over them. But it shall not be so among you; but whoever would be great among you must be your servant, and whoever would be first among you must be slave of all. For the Son of Man also came not to be served but to serve and to give His life as a ransom for many.[53]

As was the case in the Gospel of John, Mark also depicts Jesus as reversing the order of things. Once again, the greatest one is the slave of all and critiques worldly authority. James' and John's request to sit at Jesus' side presupposes ranking. Moreover, they are not the only disciples who have interpreted Jesus' power in this way. The rest of the disciples are indignant because each had coveted the same positions that James and John had requested. That this is at least Mark's interpretation is indicated by Jesus' response: Jesus addresses the twelve—not just James and John—with the words, "You know that those who are supposed to rule over the Gentiles Lord it over them, . . . *but it shall not be so among you;* but whoever would be great among you must be your servant and whoever would be greatest among you must be slave of all." Once again there is an indication of the type of power bestowed on the ordained. In terms of the world, the ordained may be understood as the "great ones" in the Church. If this is so, the authority and power bestowed upon these great ones is the authority of service and self-emptying. The ordained are to be slaves of all if they are to be the greatest. Jesus did not grant His apostles authority to "Lord it over" the people of God, and when those in the succession of the Apostles assume such worldly authority, they violate the Lord's command. Indeed, there are no promises associated with the employment of worldly power because Jesus cannot even grant such power. The statement, " . . . To sit at my right or my left is not mine to give . . . " may be true because the power that Jesus gives is different.

Since the rite of ordination does something—i.e., it bestows a charism—it is easy to confuse this rite with a sacrament. After all, sacraments also do something. The Lord's Supper forgives sins and strengthens us for Christian living in the world. Baptism saves. Confession and absolution forgive sins. But unlike the sacraments of the Supper, Baptism, and possibly Confession and Absolution, ordination is not a sacrament. The validity of the sacraments does not depend on those who preside. Any baptism done in the name of the Triune God is a baptism regardless of who presides. Likewise, the validity of the Eucharist is not undermined by the one who presides, but the rite of ordination always directs our attention toward the ones who actually perform the rite. If the guys who hang out at the bar on the corner ordain me to the Gospel ministry, there may well be some question about the validity of my ordination. Likewise, there is some question about my ordination if my mother ordains me. Who ordains is a far more important question than who baptizes in the sense that the validity of the ordination hinges on this question.

It is now appropriate to discuss apostolic succession. The Church has developed the notion of apostolic succession to safeguard the rite of ordination. Historically, there has obviously been some question about what constitutes apostolic succession. The Orthodox and Roman Catholic churches interpret apostolic succession materialistically. That is to say that they believe that their priests are validly ordained because there is an historical continuity between the apostles and their priests that is established by the laying on of hands from the apostles through each generation of priests until now. Others cannot interpret apostolic succession so literally because they know that such continuity is not historically verifiable. This has forced them to develop a theory that argues that a valid ordination is done by someone who is in the Spirit of the apostles. Obviously, many churches of the Reformation advanced such an argument because they can point to the time and place where the alleged continuity with the apostles was broken.

Those who reject the traditional, materialistic definition of apostolic succession—either because they know that continuity has been broken or because they now realize that such materialistic continuity is not historically verifiable—, might understand apostolic succession in terms of apostolic authority and power. In that case, apostolic succession must be discerned rather than assumed. (It can be discerned by determining whether or not the power and authority bestowed by an ordination rite are worldly power or the power and authority of servants.) If the power and authority are derived from death's authority, the ordination is not in the spirit of the apostles.

Indeed, there is currently a great gap between the power and authority bestowed on the apostles and that which appears to be bestowed on today's ordinands. The apostles are sent. They are told to "Go to all nations . . . ." Generally speaking, today's ordinands are "installed" into some office. If Apostolic succession depends on the bestowal of the same power and authority Jesus bestows on His apostles, our ordination into offices is appropriate only if these "offices" are the servants' quarters.

The difficulty is obvious. Through apostolic succession, Jesus grants the ordained His power and authority, and the Church often has no use for such nonsense. Those who do rely on Jesus' power and authority are up against some formidable opposition when they try to restructure the Church in accord with the power and authority of Jesus. The opposition is so formidable because our very language does not recognize the existence of any power other than the worldly power that is grounded in death. Webster's Dictionary, for example, describes power as "the ability to act . . . control others . . . sway, . . . influence, physically force."[54] This definition of power suggests that all power originates from some center and is directed against a world of objects. The only question that definition of power appears to pose is, "Am I going to be your object or are you going to be mine." From a Christian perspective this definition is even more interesting because of what it does not say. There is no mention of power being the capacity to suffer or be influenced by another. There is no inkling of power being related to self-emptying and love.[55] This is amusing, because the type of power that is *not* mentioned at all is the very sort of power that Jesus has been given and bestows on us—and we call Jesus omnipotent.

Fortunately, the power the dictionary defines is not the only power there is. In an address titled "Two Kinds of Power,"[56] Bernard Loomer distinguishes between two types: unilateral power and relational power. While unilateral power bears some resemblance to what we have called worldly power, his description of unilateral power bears repeating because it goes into more depth. Unilateral power is "the capacity to influence, guide, adjust, manipulate, shape, control, or transform the human or natural environment in order to advance one's own purposes."[57] Unilateral power is one-dimensional because it involves moving and influencing others without being subject to the influence of others. Accordingly, inequality is an inherent feature of unilateral power. Since those who influence are superior to those whom they influence, issues of status and station arise; one's rank becomes one of the more important issues. If unilateral power governs, equality cannot possibly happen. Moreover, those who possess unilateral power seldom relinquish it voluntarily. Doing so would be the same as making oneself inferior, for if one's dignity and status as a human being depend on one's superior position, the voluntary relinquishment of that position would deprive one of dignity. Under the rubric of unilateral power, concessions are made only when a rival with enough power forces an issue.[58] This may be why organizations established according to the dictates of unilateral power are often forced to institutionalize competing factions if they are concerned about issues of equality. Our more "liberal" institutions, therefore, take Saul Alinsky's astute observation concerning unilateral power quite seriously. It was Alinsky who recognized that people having unilateral power will listen only when the opposition has enough political clout to make them listen. No matter how "liberal," all organizations that operate on the basis of unilateral power promote oppression.

If we state a corollary to Alinsky's contention that people with unilateral power will listen only when the opposition has enough political clout to make them listen, the oppression present at the very core of unilateral power can be recognized. The corollary is: the powerful will remain indifferent to people who can safely be ignored.[59] The voiceless ones can be safely ignored under even the most liberal employment of unilateral power because the voiceless ones are, to use a Biblical phrase, "the least of these." Since the "least of these" can safely be ignored by those holding unilateral power, it is safe to say that unilateral power is non-communal. It is non-communal in several respects. First, it promotes conversation only between people of similar rank or positions. Under conditions where a person is either the object of those above or treats those below as objects, the only possible conversation respecting the integrity of the other person is between people occupying similar rank.

Second, unilateral power prevents communication of any sort between the powerful and "the least of these." Since the powerful remain indifferent to those who can safely be ignored, unilateral power ignores those who do not have power. We who hold unilateral power can systematically and unreflectively avoid the poor like the rich man routinely avoided Lazarus.

In the final analysis unilateral power is non-communal because it avoids fellowship with Jesus. Since Jesus promised to be in the midst of the least of these, anything that excludes the least of these excludes Jesus. Since unilateral power does this both in fact and in principle, it rejects communion with Jesus.

Fortunately, unilateral power is not the only kind of power possible. Even the Augsburg Confession recognizes this in article 28. In its discussion of the power of the bishops, article 28 contends that while unilateral power may be necessary in the world, the Church and its bishops have no business employing unilateral power because their power and authority reside in a different source. "Temporal authority is concerned with matters altogether different from the Gospel. Temporal power does not protect the soul, but with sword and physical penalties it protects the body and goods from the power of others."[60] In other words, the confessional documents of the Lutheran church encourage the question, "What sort of power ought to operate in the Church?" even though they assume, perhaps falsely, that unilateral, worldly power is always the way power must be exercised in the temporal realm.

The whole people of God, including the ordained, are thus challenged to develop an understanding of power that is not derived from the necessities imposed by this worldly sort of power. We must take the Lordship of Christ as our point of departure, and we must never confuse Christ's Lordship with that of worldly power.

The sort of power the Church might try to employ is discussed by Peter Paris in his book *The Social Teaching of the Black Churches*. Relying on Bernard Loomer's description of "relational power," Paris finds what he calls "communal power" operating within the Black Churches in the United States. Paris contends that communal power is the capacity to influence and be influenced by others. Communal power is a force which recognizes the primacy of community and the potential of the community to promote and enrich the world.[61] Communal power is not passive.[62] It is a power that resides in the community and not in the self alone. It is a power of a community to change itself, its members and the community at-large. One of the important examples of communal power that Paris cites is the civil rights movement of the 50's and 60's.

> C. Eric Lincoln argues that the decisive difference between the Montgomery bus boycott and the history of black churches is that the black religious leaders for the first time challenged the white establishment over something specific, in which one side or the other had to emerge as victor. The victory that blacks

> achieved in that event was unprecedented and it changed the whole history of the black struggle for racial justice to say nothing of its psychological impact on all who participated directly or indirectly. That type of activity enabled blacks to become initiators of action rather than respondents. In that event we see black religious leaders utilizing communal power in its full sense, that is, aiming at producing an effect and undergoing an effect, and both in the interest of enhancing community.[63]

The Montgomery boycott is an important example of how communal power once opposed the unilateral power exercised in the segregation policies of the United States. It is hardly passive. It is clearly a manifestation of power, but it is different from unilateral power because its practitioners do not simply produce an effect. They undergo an effect. They are changed by the very process they initiate.

Communal power is often practiced by the politically weak against the politically strong. To some extent, this is the only way communal power can be exercised at least until it is identified. Moreover, it becomes clear that apostolic continuity certainly resides in these black churches, since we can clearly see them manifesting the power and authority Jesus bestows.

White churches are different. The ordained in such churches are often the beneficiaries of unilateral power. If we are to live in accord with this alternative understanding of power, we must first decline these benefits. Peter Paris has done us the service of describing what an alternative to unilateral power might be. We, who employ unilateral power, must now reject it, and, since the rejection of unilateral power is often perceived as the loss of our very dignity and humanity, what is required of us is nothing more or less than our death. Like the Lord we claim to follow, we must take up this particular cross. We must recognize, with the Apostle Paul, that our baptism demands this because those who are baptized into Christ Jesus are baptized into His death. This means that we are dead to the world, with all its trappings like the benefits of unilateral power. Our baptism enables us to risk death because our baptism empowers us to live in Christ, or, as Paul says, "We were buried therefore with him by baptism into death, so that as Christ was raised from the dead by the glory of the Father, we too might walk in newness of life."[64]

Within the white churches in North America one group that benefits from unilateral power is the ordained. The ordained must die to the claims of unilateral power and, with the help of the whole people of God, begin to discover the authority and power that is in accord with the power and authority Jesus bestows. Such a discovery depends on our dying. We must die to the world and its claims that the source of life rests in unilateral power and the prestige, position, happiness, security and money that this idol bestows. Consistent with our baptism into Christ's death, we need to recognize the possible suffering that using the power and authority Jesus bestows might necessitate. But also consistent with our baptism is the fact that in our baptism into Christ we may walk in newness of life. This stroll in life's newness implies the development of new understanding and different uses of authority and power because our Lord bestows a particular type of power and authority, and it is not unilateral power.

THE ORDINATION OF WOMEN

The ordination of women is rejected in many churches. The majority of Christians are members of churches that refuse to ordain women and that have begun to develop traditions rationalizing this refusal. Questions concerning the ecumenical implications of women's ordination are raised even in church bodies that ordain women as if the ordination of women were the only serious stumbling block to Christian unity. If, however, the ordination of women is removed from false contexts—the false allegation that women have secondary status in creation, the claim that women are excluded because they are biologically dissimilar to Jesus, and the question of Christian unity—and if it is placed in the proper context of the authority and power that Jesus bestows on all believers, a clearer picture of the theological issues emerges. The theology that supports the ordination of women is as simple as it is clear: since the power and authority that Jesus bestows on his brothers and sisters has characteristics that we normally describe as being feminine, ordaining women is not a problem. Indeed, ordaining men is more theologically problematic.

In what is clearly one of the best discussions of the authority and power of life in contrast to the authority and power of death, Raine Eisler in *The Chalice and the Blade* makes some quite sweeping and interesting claims about the character of the human enterprise.[65] She begins by distinguishing between two models of social relationships which she, on occasion, calls the dominator model and the partnership model. In the dominator model, social relationships are based upon ranking. Such ranking can consist of white people being ranked above black people, adults above children, masters above slaves, employers above employees. In Eisler's well-argued opinion the fundamental ranking that forms the basis of the dominator model is the ranking of men above women. In contrast to the dominator model, the partnership model is based upon the principle of linking rather than ranking. Here human diversity is not equated with inferiority or superiority. Human diversity is merely accepted as a given.[66] The unilateral relationships that rank one person over another, characteristic of the dominator model, are replaced by the relationship of mother and child which is the paradigmatic relationship in the partnership model.

To those of us who are so ingrained and brainwashed by the dominator model, it is quite difficult to even entertain the notion that this so-called partnership model is possible. Many believe it to be nothing but a utopian dream. This is why Eisler finds it necessary to argue that the partnership model was once nearly universal and that the dominator model we currently experience is but a 5000 year deviation from the norm. Accordingly, Eisler reinterprets archeological evidence and comes to understand the life of our predecessors in remarkably new ways. Her conclusion is that we once were organized according to a partnership model which was replaced by a dominator model at a much more recent date.[67]

At least one observation about Eisler's theory is quite significant for this discussion concerning the ordination of women. According to her theory, the partnership model gives women a central position in the social order without recourse to matriarchy. Eisler convincingly demonstrates that matriarchy is the one conceivable alternative to patriarchy only if the dominator model is in force in the first place. Only if we mistakenly assume that society must be structured on the basis of ranking, and note that men are not in a position of dominance will we think that the only alternative to patriarchy is matriarchy.[68] However, if we recognize that the authority that gives power to the partnership model is the authority of life, and the authority that bestows power on the dominator model is the authority of death, then we may find it possible to envision alternatives to both patriarchy and matriarchy.

The power of life cannot kill and still be supreme. Therefore any social order structured according to the authority and power of life will hold central those things that it understands to give and nurture life. To be sure, what some think central to life may not actually be so, but societies organized according to the partnership model will attempt to place that which they deem most life-giving at the center. This is the reason for women's central place in cultures that predate the dominator model. Women most obviously give life. They most obviously nurture life. In a culture that derives its authority from life, women will be central. The centrality of women, however, does not mean that men are ranked lower than women. Indeed, the partnership model has no ranking at all. Men also participate in life. They are partners, not inferiors. The partnership model is both female centered and life-giving, and, as such, it is more consistent with the power of Jesus than is the dominator model. It is also far more feminine. As a result, the partnership model also illustrates how, if ordination is discussed in terms of the power and authority Jesus bestows, the ordination of men is far more problematic than the ordination of women. The partnership model quite successfully links life to the feminine, and has remarkable similarities with the power and authority Jesus bestows. The partnership model also suggests that the ordination of men is not impossible even though it may well be more problematic. The reason is simple: the opposite of patriarchy is matriarchy only if the dominator model is assumed. If the partnership model is assumed, all human beings are enlisted in the support of life, and, accordingly, men can exhibit many of the characteristics and qualities often described as feminine. Today, however, when men exhibit such qualities they do so in spite of our current culture.

Those who employ the power and authority of Jesus are more concerned with small things than with grand schemes and designs. This is true because life is more often found in small things than it is in grand designs. This is not to say that global issues are unimportant. It is merely to say that global issues are important because of their effect on that which is counted small. If we begin with small things, and discuss global issues in so far as they serve the small, it will be far less likely that we will sacrifice these little ones to some grand design that is opposed to life.

In any case, Jesus is often shown as acting on behalf of the little ones. At a time when children had few rights and mere contact with a child undermined a man's respectability, Jesus commands his disciples to bring the children to Him that He might bless them.[69] We might pause here for a moment to note that those who first brought the children to Jesus, most probably women, indicated by their actions that they knew more than the disciples about the power and authority of Jesus. In their attempt to send the children away, the disciples were concerned about Jesus' social status, and they understood His status to be based upon the dictates of unilateral power. The women who challenged the disciples may well have understood Jesus much better because they recognized that His power and authority supported what the world deemed to be unimportant.

In the Gospel of Mark, Jesus actually identifies Himself with children. The disciples, who still interpret Jesus in terms of unilateral power and the dominator model, are arguing about who is the greatest among them. Jesus says, "If anyone would be first, he must be last of all and servant of all." In saying this He seems to be rejecting unilateral power. Then, as a demonstration of this rejection, it is written, " . . . He took a child, put him in the midst of them; and taking him in His arms, He said to them, 'Whoever receives one such child in my name receives me, and whoever receives me receives not me but Him who sent me.' "[70] To disassociate Himself from worldly rule, Jesus turns to a child. He does so not only to demonstrate His opposition to unilateral power, but to disestablish unilateral power and the dominator model, for if Jesus is Lord, authority and power are different. When Jesus promises to be present whenever a child is received in His name, He promises to be with His followers whenever they oppose forces seeking to destroy "the little ones." Here Jesus has joined this struggle for life by identifying with mothers throughout history, who had no choice but to lay down their lives for their children. That such self-giving power is normally associated with feminine characteristics is important, but more important is how Jesus subverts the world when He embodies this authority and power.

The fact that the Church is far more comfortable employing the unilateral power in the dominator model than it is in the use of the power and authority of Jesus is so obvious that it is hardly worth mentioning. Less obvious, however, is that our fascination with unilateral power has greatly contributed to our refusal to ordain women.[71] According to Jacques Ellul, it is our accommodation to unilateral power and the "benefits" of the dominator model that has led to the subversion of Christianity. Christianity has been mesmerized by the principalities and powers and has adopted their ways. Christianity has accommodated itself to that which "works." The Church has associated with the strong at the expense of the weak. We prefer the big to the small.[72] Ellul often makes the point that Christianity's preferences, associations, and accommodations that have subverted it have also led to what can only be described as anti-feminine. In other words, Ellul contends that the anti-feminine character of what we now call Christianity is a consequence of Christianity's subversion, and much of Christianity's subversion is due to our accommodation to unilateral power.

> Our only reproach against the Church leaders and theologians is that they set about justifying and

legitimating the powers by trying to show that there is no contradiction, particularly between wealth and Jesus, using the (undeniable) strand in the Old Testament that treats riches as a tangible proof of divine blessing. The worm was in the fruit. The theological betrayal consisted of demonstrating that this was not a worm. But now it all held together. Once a stitch broke, however, everything began to unravel. Once the poor were, of course still well received and supported and served in the Church, but after the manner we have said, all that represented weakness of inferiority (physical, social etc.) was put in second place.

Women are the most spectacular instance of this. After a period of independence that came with the spread of Christianity, they were relegated to a lower order. This is all the more interesting because the gospel and the first church were never hostile to women nor treated them as minors . . . . In spite of this, when Christianity became a power or authority, this worked against women. A strange perversion, yet fully understandable when we allow that women represent precisely the most innovative elements in Christianity: grace, love, charity, a concern for living creatures, non-violence, an interest in little things, the hope for new beginnings—the very elements that Christianity was setting aside in favor of glory and success . . . .

Christianity took this course by reason of the mutation that led it to adopt the values of conquest, power, and dominion (in a good cause!). Since then women have been debarred from participation in the spiritual life and in the truth of Christ.[73]

The dominator model with its intimate link to unilateral power is always contrary to those characteristics described as feminine. It prefers principles to people. It favors the strong over the weak. It supports the illusion of autonomy over the reality of our inter-dependence in community. When the Church accommodates itself to the dominator model, it becomes anti-feminine because feminine qualities are not consistent with the power of the dominator model. The dominator model receives its authority and power from death, and, to a large extent, the qualities we often call feminine receive their power from life.[74]

Christians continue to subvert Christianity to the extent that they refuse to use the power and authority our Lord has bestowed upon us. Until we do so—until we refrain from the uncritical adoption of the dominator model in human relationships—we will remain instruments of death rather than life. Our refusal to use the power our Lord bestows means that we must seek our destiny among idols. The Church's adoption of unilateral power is indicative of idol worship. Unilateral power gets its authority from these idols which, in their turn, derive their authority from death. The fact that death is the ultimate authority of the dominator model and the unilateral power it exercises accounts for many of the characteristics of the social arrangements that occur under this model. For example, the fact that victims of unilateral power are turned into objects by those who exercise power over them is indicative of death's ultimate authority in the dominator model. Objects are devoid of life. If a living thing is treated as an object, it is being treated as if it were dead because a living thing dies when it becomes a mere object. Unilateral power is definitely a power, but it gets its authority from death. Its link to death is beyond dispute.[75] That the Church has often been an instrument of death is also beyond dispute. We have had and continue to have inquisitions, wars and public torture in the name of Jesus. We continue to silence people who are at odds with "orthodox" views, and we do most of these things because we have accommodated ourselves to the dictates of unilateral power.

But even in the midst of all these attempts to subvert Christianity, a Church within the "church" has always existed. It is not the invisible Church that many theologians have said resides unseen within the institutional churches—this Church has always been quite visible. But we who have uncritically accepted the dominator model in our human relationships, do not, as a rule, see this very visible Church. This Church has been composed chiefly of the poor and of women. In the United States, this Church has been alive and well in black churches. From time to time, it even receives a convert or two from among those who have grown accustomed to the dominator model. Men like St. Francis and Bartolome de las Casas are examples of such converts. This church has acted in accord with the power and authority Jesus bestows. Members of this Church have usually focused on what some might call insignificant things: defense of the poor, widows, children. Moreover they have done so without fanfare. Those who minister in this Church often remain unrecognized despite the vital tasks they perform. Adherents of unilateral power try to prevent their recognition, but this effort has been less than successful. Most everyone who has been among the people of God knows people who are members of this Church.

Bonnie Bowman Thurston, in the preface to her new book *The Widows: A Women's Ministry in the Early Church*, speaks about the seeming invisibility of such very visible people. Her own observations about widows occasioned this study.

> In 1983 a number of magazines ran feature articles on the world's fastest growing poverty group: women. In the United States the poorest group of all was elderly

women who had been homemakers and who as widows, had no pensions or health coverage. The statistics I read were particularly striking because I observed in churches I served and visited that it was often this very group of older women who were carrying the primary burden of service to and support of their congregations. I was troubled by the apparent contradiction between the statistics I read and the reality I saw. And so this study was born.

My first line of inquiry was to see how older women were treated in the Bible. What I discovered astounded me. From Israel's earliest days, there was concern for and support of widows. The early Christian church was praised because "there was not a needy one among them" (Acts 4:34), and one of its first benevolent works was for widows (Acts 6:1-7). The Church not only supported needy widows but by the second century it elevated them to the status of a clerical order. That order was the most prominent group of women in the first three centuries of the church. The widows as a recognized group were referred to by all major church orders. Yet no book-length study had been devoted to the widows and their order.[76]

One way to account for our total disregard for the widows as a clerical order—and for their "invisibility" within our church bodies—is our preoccupation with unilateral power and the dominator model. We have already noticed that this preoccupation may well be due to a preoccupation with the authority and power of death rather than life. As a consequence, the fact that we do not see what has been before our eyes is indicative of our refusal to use the authority and power Jesus bestows. In any case, it is in keeping with this ongoing struggle between death and life that the powers of death may well try to destroy ministries that receive their authority from Jesus. It is in keeping with Jesus' victory over death that these ministries have not been destroyed.

Those who employ unilateral power have been trying to destroy the power and authority that God bestows at least since the formation of Scripture; but, since it is God's power and authority that is under attack, these efforts have not succeeded. That such efforts have been made, however, is undeniable.[77]

The infancy narratives of Moses may illustrate the failure of all attempts to interpret Moses, the political leader of Israel, in terms of the dominator model.

> Then the king of Egypt said to the Hebrew midwives, one of whom was named Shiph'rah and the other Puah, "When you serve as midwife to the Hebrew women, and see them upon the birth stool, if it is a son, you shall kill him; but if it is a daughter, she shall live." But the midwives feared God and did not do as the king of Egypt commanded them, but let the male children live. So the king of Egypt called the midwives, and said to them, "Why have you done this, and let the male children live?" The midwives said to the Pharaoh, "Because the Hebrew women are not like the Egyptian women; for they are vigorous, and are delivered before the midwife comes to them. . . ." Then the Pharaoh commanded all his people, "Every son that is born to the Hebrew you shall cast into the Nile, but you shall let every daughter live."

> Now a man from the house of Levi went and took a wife, a daughter of Levi. The woman conceived and bore a son; and when she saw that he was a goodly

> child, she hid him for three months. And when she could hide him no longer, she took for him a basket made of bulrushes, and daubed it with bitumen and pitch; and she put the child in it and placed it among the reeds at the river's brink. And his sister stood at a distance to know what would be done to him. Now the daughter of the Pharaoh came down to bathe at the river, and her maidens walked beside the river; she saw the basket among the reeds and sent her maid to fetch it. When she opened it she saw the child; and lo, the babe was crying. She took pity on him and said, "This is one of the Hebrews' children." Then his sister said to Pharaoh's daughter, "Shall I go and call you a nurse from the Hebrew women to nurse the child for you?" And the Pharaoh's daughter said to her, "Go." So the girl went and called the child's mother. And the Pharaoh's daughter said to her, "Take this child away, and nurse him for me, and I will give you your wages." So the woman took the child and nursed him. And the child grew, and she brought him to Pharaoh's daughter, and he became her son; and she named him Moses, for she said, "Because I drew him out of the water."[78]

This narrative is dominated by women who all perform tasks that are remarkably courageous and prove vital to Israel's survival. Women perform these tasks because they exhibited concern for what many adherents of the dominator model might call "little things," and, in this context, it is the "little things" that are the source of life. In the first story, the Pharaoh orders two midwives named Shiph'rah and Puah to kill all male children born to Hebrew women. Alice L. Laffey has pointed out the irony of this command. "Shiphrah and Puah could allow the female infants to live because women could never become powerful enough or important enough to threaten Egyptian security," and yet it is two women who undermine that security by disobeying the Pharaoh's order.[79] Attentiveness to the babies and children undermines Pharaoh's power. Shiph'rah and Puah are heroines because they refused to be instruments of death. They are probably mere footnotes in this story because those who finally wrote this account may well have written from the same perspective as Pharaoh held when he ordered the slaughter of all male infants. Nevertheless, the vital role of Shiph'rah and Puah cannot be denied. It can only be ignored by those of us who have grown very accustomed to the dominator model. Normally, we focus instead on the glorious Red Sea battle that serves as a climax to this story, and we disregard the little things that may have made the battle and subsequent victory possible.

The attempt to undermine the identity of women may also be operative in the account of Moses' birth. In this account two important women are not named, even though it is reasonable to assume that their names were quite well known. The first is Jochebed, the unnamed mother of Moses (Exodus 6:20; Numbers 26:59). In this narrative the unnamed mother courageously hides her son for three months and then places him in a basket and puts the basket at the river's edge. Under the watchful eyes of her unnamed daughter Miriam(?), Moses is discovered by the Pharaoh's daughter. Pharaoh's daughter then, in violation of her father's order to kill all male Hebrew infants, took pity on the baby, and Moses' unnamed but quite ingenious sister not only manages to get her mother to nurse Moses, but she arranges to have her mother paid for the privilege. Once again, the roles of two or possibly three women are so vital to the story that they cannot be overlooked. All along their focus is on the child. Their efforts give this one little one life, and Israel is saved as a consequence. This, of course, is indicative of the power and authority that God bestows on His people. It is the power and authority of life. As such, it must touch and preserve the living in the face of the other powers that serve death.

Hebrew Scriptures are not the only place where the attempt to ignore those who employ the power that God bestows is unsuccessful. In the New Testament, we try to disregard the fact that women were not only among Jesus' first followers, but were probably the first witnesses to His resurrection. We often overlook the possibility that women were included among the disciples themselves (Acts 9:36). Disregard for the pivotal role of women in Scripture has been the norm throughout Church history and is widespread today, despite the fact that it can easily be argued that women have always been more likely to use the power and authority that Jesus bestows.

We must admit that the ordained often fail to use the authority and power bestowed upon them in their baptism and ordination. We must also admit that the ordained have usually preferred to use unilateral power and have been predisposed to adopt the authority of death. The ordination of women, therefore, must be discussed in the context of the authority and power Jesus bestows. Rather than being a threat to ecumenical dialogue or church union, as is sometimes argued, the ordination of women is testimony to the fact that God's reality, authority, and power cannot be denied forever. There is Gospel in the fact of the ordination of women. Let us recognize it!

WHO SHALL BE ORDAINED?

The fact that the power and authority Jesus bestows have characteristics usually associated with the feminine does not mean that all baptized women should be ordained—no matter how fascinating that would make the Church. All it means is that the ordination of women is quite consistent with the power and authority Jesus bestows. It is now important to consider which women (and perhaps men) should be ordained. Given the nature of our discussion, the answer is simple in principle, but far more difficult in practice. Good candidates for ordination are those whose calling and vocation routinely place them in the position of performing those tasks that create arenas in which the Body of Christ can discern Jesus' presence, testify to that presence, and follow. These tasks have been discussed elsewhere in this study, but a brief review of them may now be in order.

In I Timothy 4:12-14 it is written, "Till I come, attend to the public reading of Scripture, to preaching, to teaching. Do not neglect the gift you have which was given you by prophetic utterance when the council of elders laid their hands upon you. Practice these duties, devote yourself to them, so that all may see your progress." Attending to public reading of Scripture (read worship), to preaching and teaching are ways to avoid neglecting the charism ordination bestows. Moreover, if this gift actually is the promise of Christ's presence and power in arenas created by these tasks, then it is in the interest of the Body of Christ to ordain those whose vocation routinely involves them in performing such tasks because the charism bestowed at ordination works only in such arenas.

A list of candidates for ordination can be developed from this analysis of I Timothy. This list is short and does not include missionaries, who would certainly be included if the discussion turned to an analysis of the apostolic commission. If we limit the discussion to I Timothy, the list of possible candidates who it might be to the Church's advantage to ordain might include: pastors serving congregations, organists, choir directors, cantors, teachers, bishops and seminarians. These are included because these callings routinely involve performing the tasks that create arenas for the discernment of

Jesus' presence. Pastors are obviously included on this list because they are routinely involved in worship, preaching and teaching. Since organists, choir directors, and cantors are routinely involved in leading worship in their efforts to fulfill their calling, it might be in the interest of the Church to ordain these people too, particularly if the charism ordination bestows is taken seriously. The Church can bestow this charism on whoever it is in the interest of the Church to give it, and it is in the interest of the Church to make sure that those whose vocational tasks routinely place them in arenas cleared for discernment actually receive this charism. By the same token, it may also be in the interest of the Church to ordain those seminary students who routinely preach, lead worship, and teach as part of their seminary education, if the Church makes such a determination.

Now, it is clear that such a list of candidates for ordination has its problems, but some of these problems may well be caused by our preconceived notions of what constitutes ordination. For many, ordination is linked to gainful employment rather than to vocation. If that link is made, then the conclusion may be that seminarians and those concerned with church music should not be ordained because seminarians are not gainfully employed and directors of music are not paid enough. Such a conclusion, however, is based more on economic reasoning than on theological grounds.

Others may have difficulty with this list of candidates for ordination because it is difficult to pack all these candidates into some preconceived structure of ordained ministry. It is quite difficult to apply something like the three-fold structure—bishop, pastor, and deacon—to all the candidates listed. Are seminarians deacons? Technically speaking they are not. They are seminarians. Are ministers of music deacons? Not really. In reality they are ministers of music. These people should simply be called what they are.

Forget the traditional terminology. Indeed, when that terminology was introduced, those who employed it were merely calling people what they were. They did not invent the categories.

This fact is quite evident in I Timothy which is certainly one source for the view that the ordained ministry must have a three-fold structure. The author of I Timothy first names the office of bishop and attempts to list some expectations for that office (I Timothy 3:1-7). The office of bishop was not invented by I Timothy. It existed already when I Timothy was written. Deacons are recognized, and some expectations are listed (I Timothy 3: 8-13). Then the author does the same with pastors. In the process, the author delineates what we now call the three-fold office. Interestingly enough, however, I Timothy itself is not limited to this three-fold structure. After discussing expectations for pastors, I Timothy discusses widows as if they too were some kind of office. "Let a widow be *enrolled* if she is not less than sixty years of age . . . ." (I Timothy 5:9). Moreover, I Timothy 5:3 tells us to honor widows who are real widows. Bonnie Thurston tells us that the Greek word for honor (*tima*) can also mean pay or compensate, and in the later church orders *timan* was a technical term for payment.[80] Be that as it may, in the context of I Timothy it appears that the author is merely recognizing legitimate ministries and calling them what they were. It was only later that we baptized these descriptions of existing ministries and tried to squeeze our more contemporary forms of ministry into this structure.

The issue of who is to be ordained—particularly as the Church intentionally enters the post-Constantinian era—should be settled by discerning those vocations or callings that routinely involve their practitioner in worship, preaching, teaching, and mission. Since the vocations of some church musicians, seminarians, and others routinely place them in such positions, it might be in the interest of the Church to ordain them. It is true that this would create some new difficulties, but it might not create any more difficulty than we already have. Nonetheless, there are some practical considerations that are appropriate.

When the issue of who is to be ordained is moved to individual cases, the Church once again finds that discernment is necessary, since it faces the task of discerning a person's calling. It is in the interest of the Church to ordain only those people whose *vocation* or *calling* places them in positions where they perform those tasks which create arenas in which discernment occurs. We must here distinguish between a job description and a calling, for, not everyone who plays the organ in a church or studies Christianity is called. What happens, for example, if we ordain all church organists and a church organist turns out to be a heretic or an atheist? What happens if a particular seminarian cannot or does not desire to be a pastor? What do we do with our Sunday School teachers or those who teach God's Word in the schools we establish? The necessity to discern is obvious. Our ultimate determination probably should be based on whether the practices in which our candidates are routinely involved in pursuit of their vocation leads them to routinely deal with worship, preaching, teaching, or mission in such a way that Jesus' presence can be discerned, witnessed, and followed by those believers who assemble where Jesus has promised to be.

Chapter Four

The Priesthood of All Believers

As long as we prefer worldly power to the power and authority Jesus bestows, we will pay only lip service to one of the more radical notions of the Reformation: the priesthood of all believers. The slogan "priesthood of all believers" was employed by Luther and other sixteenth century reformers in order to express the rather innovative notion that all believers were priest, bishop and pope by virtue of their baptism. All of the baptized are called to be ministers of the God who became flesh in Jesus Christ, and all are disciples of Jesus in the contexts into which they have been called.

Very early in this inquiry, it was noted that this notion of the priesthood of all believers was undermined by some of the events of the Reformation. In opposition to some of their own confessional documents that insist on the difference between temporal authority and the authority that Church officials must employ,[81] many churches of the Reformation began to formulate the relationship between Church and state in ways consistent with the Constantinian structures of the past. Some reformers sought the favor of Princes. Others established states that sanctioned certain civil authorities. Bowing to political realities, Lutherans even agreed that the Prince's religious preference would become the religion of the land, despite their contention that the individual believer was justified by faith rather than national origin. In the course of these events, Protestant Christianity, particularly Lutherans and Reformed, uncritically accepted the dominator model of human relationships with its marked preference for unilateral power. With unilateral power as the norm, relations between the people of God and the clergy could not be mutually edifying. One group would have to "lord it over" the other. At certain times and places, it was the people of God who dominated, and in other places and times the clergy achieved a superior position. In either case, the dominant factor was the Constantinian background that we had uncritically appropriated. We had appropriated this model when we accepted worldly power.

This presentation has tried to outline a theology of ministry against a different background. An analysis of the theology of the ministry of the people of God remains. Such ministries are a challenge to say the least for they too involve dying so that we might walk in newness of life.

THE MINISTRY OF THE PEOPLE OF GOD

The ministry of the whole people of God is similar to those ministries that we normally associate with the ordained. The purpose of the ordained ministry is to discern the presence of Jesus in media in which Jesus has promised to be, to witness to that presence, and to follow Jesus. The purpose of ministries we normally associate with the people of God is to discern the presence of Jesus in media in which Jesus has not promised to be but goes nonetheless, to witness to that presence, and to follow. In both cases, discernment, witness, and discipleship are constitutive of ministry. It is the media in which these ministries occur that distinguish the ordained ministry from the ministries of the people of God. The actual principles that are constitutive of ministry are not different. In whatever context Christians find themselves, their task is to discern Jesus' presence, to testify to that presence, and to follow.

To repeat this important assertion, it is the media in which a particular ministry occurs that distinguish the ministries commonly associated with the ordained from those ministries normally associate with the priesthood of all believers. As we have seen, the ministries of the ordained occur in contexts created by the tasks we normally associate with the ordained. These include: preaching, sacraments, "wherever two or three are gathered in Jesus' name," "the least of these," receiving a child in Jesus' name, mission, teaching, etc. Moreover, all of these and perhaps more are at least candidates for media in which Jesus has promised to be present.

It has also been noted that Jesus is not confined to these media. Just as any human being's presence is not limited to the places where he or she has promised to be, so it is with Jesus. Jesus is alive! Jesus is God! Jesus can go wherever He desires. Thus, the ministries of the people of God happen in media in which Jesus has not explicitly promised to be present, but may go nonetheless. As a consequence, ministry in family, business, government, art, the service industries, and many other places is possible because Jesus does not absent Himself from these places. Ministry in such places, however, does not occur automatically. A Christian can be present in family, business, government, etc., and not minister if that person views his or her primary task to be other than ministry. In other words, the primary task of a Christian in business is not to make money. The primary task of the Christian in business is to discern Jesus' presence in the realm of business, to testify to that presence, and to follow Jesus wherever Jesus may lead. If making money in business has priority over the discerning, witnessing, and following of Jesus, then that person is not intentionally doing ministry. To be sure, Jesus can minister anywhere and use any of our activities, but in such a case, Jesus ministers in spite of the intention of the person. Likewise, the primary task of a Christian parent is not to nurture children, though that is an important task. The primary task of a Christian parent is to discern Jesus presence in the realm of family life, to testify to that presence, and to follow Jesus. Obviously, this may place Christians at odds with the necessities inherent in the domain in which they find themselves; it may require them to leave the domain altogether; it may even require dying.

To complicate matters further, the people of God are always tempted to identify the necessities inherent in a particular domain with ministry itself. A Christian parent will always be tempted to confuse the welfare of the children with Jesus. A Christian in business will always be tempted to confuse earning money with the task of discipleship. A Christian politician will always be tempted to place election to office above faithfulness to Jesus. Such are the temptations of ministry in media in which Jesus has not promised to be present but is present nonetheless. Temptations abound as Jesus' disciples act in the world for the purpose of ministering. This should not be too much of a surprise, because temptation was a constant companion of Jesus Himself as He ministered in the world.

Since the people of God are tempted by the necessities present in the domains within which they are called to minister, it is appropriate to describe these necessities.[82] The word necessity is not to be equated with something that is strictly determined. A necessity is something that need not be done, but, given the nature of the particular context in which a person operates, it will very probably be done. In other words, a necessity is something you *don't have to do,* but you will. In the United States and Canada we don't have to buy presents at Christmas for people who have absolutely no need for them, but we will. It is a social necessity. People will get angry if we do not participate in this thirty day ritual of frenzied buying.[83] A person does not have to obey the social necessity that dominates in this ritual, but disregard of this necessity would lead to suffering of some sort. At the very least, a person's friends and relatives would be angry. At the most, a family might be divided. The refusal to act in accord with even the simplest of social necessities leads to suffering.

A political necessity is another example. In the United States today it is necessary for many candidates for national offices, and many local offices, to appear on television. Everyone knows that it would be impossible for a Presidential candidate to become President if he or she refused to employ television properly. Moreover, many analysts of the television medium have shown that this medium undermines democracy because it cannot tolerate serious political debate. Just as we cannot discuss philosophy using smoke signals, we cannot debate complex issues on television because television, at least as it currently operates, is an entertainment medium that simply does not tolerate complex issues.[84] Accordingly, television imposes a political necessity on our political "debate" transforming it into slogan shouting like "Where's the beef?" and "Read my lips. No new taxes!!!" As a consequence, our national candidates in these precarious times debate issues like, "Should public school teachers be required to lead their students in the 'Pledge of Allegiance to the Flag.' " Such is the nature of political necessity. In an age of nuclear weapons, massive starvation, toxic waste, environmental destruction, over-population, conflict over abortion, racism, and sexism, it is politically necessary that our Presidential campaigns revolve around trite slogans and the opening exercises of our elementary schools. All this is politically necessary. It is obvious that we do not have to do this, but we will do this because television is the most efficient way to get elected to public office, and, as it now stands, our television medium cannot tolerate debates of important issues. They are simply too complex for this medium.

Necessities have such power because they are grounded in idolatry, and an idol is something that a person or society relies on for survival. Make no mistake. An idol need not be expressly recognized by those under its spell. Indeed, our idols often go unnoticed. They are often very close because they are equated with life itself. We uncritically adopt them because we are not capable of even recognizing that life can be lived in a different way. Like water does for fish, idols establish the context of our lives. Understood in this way, one of the closest personal analogies to an idol that I can think of is my keys. As long as my keys are in my pocket, I do not even think about them. Yet, I use them to gain access to my home, office, car and other places that are very important to me. As long as I have my keys, life is fine. But, if I lose my keys, life as I know it grinds to a standstill. I cannot drive my car. I cannot gain access to the most important places in my life. I must seek out the help of others to do my most routine task. My demeanor is altered. I am not myself. Instead of writing, reading, teaching and enjoying the company of others, I clean the house in the hope of finding what was lost. Instead of looking ahead when I walk, I find myself scanning the ground before me in the hope of finding my keys. Instead of being relatively pleasant, I am an angry man. After all, my keys are gone!!! How can life as I know it go on? This analogy between an idol and my keys serves to illustrate that an idol is often so close that we cannot recognize it until it is gone, and it illustrates how the absence of an idol may change the course of one's life.

It does not, however, illustrate the fact that idols are thought to be fundamental to life itself. This aspect of idolatry can be illustrated by an event that happened following a sermon that I preached as a guest preacher. On this occasion, I had stated that the Economy was considered by many people to be a god. A man came to me after the sermon. He had been very much upset by my associating the Economy with a god. As he left the church, he said loud enough for all to hear, "How can you even compare the Economy with a god? The Economy is the source of life! Without a good Economy we could not live! It's not a god!" Being the guest pastor, I did not point out the fact that he had just called the Economy a source of life, and that was certainly at least one quality that people attribute to their gods.

For a person, a community, or a country in which the Economy is the false god, life is inconceivable apart from economic necessities. For persons for whom sex is an idol, life is inconceivable apart from the necessities imposed on them by their sexuality. For the persons, communities, or nations who name power as their source of life, life is impossible outside the necessities imposed by the political sphere. The list of such necessities could be extended to include other biological and social necessities, but the point, I think, has been made. We act in accord with necessities because they are grounded in idolatry, and idols are thought to be the source of life.

On the other hand, we do not *have* to act in accord with a given necessity *because* necessities are grounded in idolatry and idols have no authority apart from the authority we give them. No person *has* to buy Christmas presents for people who neither need nor want them. No person *has* to use money in every day life. No person *has* to succumb to political necessities. It is clearly true that rejecting these necessities is not easy. Rejection most often results in suffering of some sort, but, if Jesus is Lord and His path is to the cross, discipleship is not without suffering.

Ministry in everyday life means violating certain necessities. Accordingly, suffering is a possibility for the one who seeks to be a minister in everyday life. All believers are called to minister within media that contain certain necessities, and that may be, as a consequence, under the dominion of certain idols. In other words, we are called to minister in the world, but we are not subject to the necessities of the world. As Paul says, we are in the world but not of the world. We are in the economic realm primarily to discern Jesus' presence, to testify to that presence, and to follow. We are not in the economic realm primarily to make money. Indeed, we may need to make money in order to remain in the economic realm. A banker without money is not a banker, and a banker without money may not be in the position to minister among his or her colleagues in banking. Nevertheless, if the economic necessity to make money takes priority over ministering, the Christian is engaged in idolatry. People who minister in everyday life must walk this kind of tightrope as they attempt to minister in the many domains that compose everyday life without succumbing to necessities.

What complicates matters further if a person is to minister is that there is no escape from this situation. Even family life involves such tensions. Some degree of honor and respect are owed our parents, and we must nurture our children. But if a mother defines herself strictly in terms of the necessities of motherhood, she will miss the fact that her primary task, in relation to her family, is to discern Jesus' presence, to witness to that presence, and to follow Jesus in the midst of family life. Such a priority could lead to sacrificing of herself, her child, her spouse or her parents in certain instances. This possibility was clearly recognized by early

Christians and more than likely by Jesus Himself as it is written:

> Do not think that I have come to bring peace on earth, I have not come to bring peace, but a sword. For I have come to set a man against his father, and daughter against her mother, and daughter-in-law against mother-in-law; and a man's foes will be those of his own household. He who loves mother and father more than me is not worthy of me; and he who does not take his cross and follow me is not worthy of me.[85]

In fact, tensions between the necessities of family life and ministry may be even more pronounced than the tension that exists between the necessities of the economic realm and ministry. The passage just quoted does not seek to circumvent this tension. It seeks to describe it. The passage ends with reference to taking up our crosses and following Jesus. Like the ordained, who have already been counseled in this study to die to the trappings and necessities of unilateral power so they might better serve the people of God, the people of God are now being challenged to take up their crosses. Suffering awaits all who do not succumb to the necessities of everyday life. Since the people of God are called to abandon the world's necessities—without at the same time abandoning the world—they will probably suffer. That is the awesome task of ministry for the people of God as they minister in media Jesus has not promised to be but is present nonetheless.

The suffering that the people of God must court in their attempts to discern Jesus' presence in the world, to witness to that presence, and to follow may have different characteristics from the suffering that the ordained are called to endure. To be sure, the cause of suffering is the same for all Christians. It is idolatry. But in places where the Church is linked with worldly power, the suffering that the ordained are called to undergo is a consequence of the attempt to abandon the benefits of worldly power. When the people of God suffer, however, it is often because they are *victims* of worldly power. A Christians's response to the idols of the world, therefore, depends upon his or her relationship to these idols. If benefits are received from the idol, it is quite permissible to understand one's ministry in terms of self-emptying. In this case, humility is a virtue to be practiced and pride is a vice to be avoided.

However, Christians who are victims of idols have a different relationship to these idols, and, as a consequence, the character of their ministry will differ. Rather than receiving benefits, these victims of idolatry suffer unnecessarily. Were *they* to "empty themselves" and humbly obey the powers that be, they would only be doing what the idols demanded. In the process, they would submit to the authority and power of death. Conditions like these require virtues quite different from humility. They require the courage to stand fast against the idol, even when threatened by death. Ministry under such circumstances is dangerous, to say the least; yet such circumstances are not foreign to the people of God who often risk their jobs, their economic security, and even their lives, in their efforts to discern, to witness, and to follow their Lord into places that Jesus has not promised to be, but is present nonetheless.

The dangerous aspects of the ministries of the priesthood of all believers are indicative of another important feature of these ministries. The ministries of the people of God are probably less communal than those we associate with the ordained. This means that the people of God often have to discern, to testify, and carry out their discipleship outside of the gathering of believers. In saying this, I do not want to minimalize the isolation that ordained ministers experience. Very often the ordained find themselves alone and think that they have to make important decisions in isolation. Sometimes this is necessary, but, in so far as ministry occurs in media in which Jesus has promised to be present, isolation need not be the normal situation. The discernment of Jesus in media where He has promised to be is best described as a corporate phenomenon. In most cases, it is not an isolated event. Perhaps much of the isolation that the ordained experience can be eliminated if they recognize the corporate dimensions of discernment in the Body of Christ. Moreover, isolated decision making on the part of the ordained may often be detrimental because it precludes a variety of spiritual gifts being brought to bear on the task at hand.

Those whose ministries are normally associated with the priesthood of all believers are much more likely to encounter legitimate isolation. They might be the only ones in their work place who are actively discerning Jesus' presence. Often they are called to discern, to witness, and to follow in environments hostile to such practices. To complicate matters further, there may be no communal support immediately available to them in such an environment. These Christians find themselves isolated precisely because of the dangers implicit in the medium in which they have been called to minister. Most people who work in the medium in which a particular Christian has been called to minister are in that medium for other reasons. Whereas the Christian is there to discern, to witness, and to follow Jesus, the Christian's co-workers are normally there because they have become subject to the necessity that governs the medium in which they are present. These two purposes could come into conflict, and the Christian might find himself or herself at odds with the entire group and called to discern in isolation. The ministries of the people of God are very often more precarious and more isolated than are the ministries of the ordained who have much communal support.

This difference between ministries of the people of God and ordained ministries can be further illustrated by an analysis of the differences between a sermon and the activity we call witnessing. Even though preaching and witnessing are actually quite similar in their structure, witnessing is normally a far more dangerous activity than preaching, at least in the United States of America. Both attempt to discern Jesus' presence. Both testify to that presence, and both should call their listeners to discipleship. But a sermon differs from witnessing in one important respect. The community to which the sermon is addressed anticipates the sermon. The people gathered expect to hear it! For some strange reason, many people actually *want* to hear it. Since the sermon has the initial support of the community it addresses, it is not an event that comes as a surprise or shock. Perhaps what is said in the sermon will be shocking, but that does not detract from the fact that the community often supports even things that are shocking.

The activity of witnessing is quite different from a sermon because it cannot count on the support of the community it addresses. Indeed, the community or person who receives this testimony may well be hostile. As a result, the one who witnesses is usually more at risk than the one who preaches. The difference between a sermon and a witness illustrates the fact that ministering in places Jesus has not promised to be is often more hazardous, for, it may be done in isolation from the community of believers. Suffice it to say that the Church should recognize the hazards of these ministries and organize itself in such a way that it can better support them. The ministries of all believers to the world are clearly fundamental to the Church; moreover, those who minister in the world are clearly at risk. The Church should organize to support these ministries so that the people of God are not left alone in the world to fight principalities and powers without the support of the Body of Christ.

THE PRIESTHOOD OF ALL BELIEVERS AND THE ORGANIZATION OF THE BODY OF CHRIST

Few tasks are theologically neutral. The organization and administration of the Church on earth certainly are not. It is becoming increasingly clear that the Church must organize in such a way that its organizational structure promotes Gospel ministry and not something else. Administrative structures that make ministry more difficult should be rejected. Just as building houses, delivering letters, or governing a nation require certain sorts of organization and exclude others, the ministries of the Gospel require certain structures and exclude others. It may well be that there are a number of possible structures to promote the Church's ministries and mission, but it is equally clear that some structures undermine the Church's mission. Not just any administrative structure will do. Some are incompatible with the Gospel and its mission.

The power and authority Jesus bestows are the power of service and love which is rooted in the God of life. It is impossible for this power to be the power of *life* if it turns the focus of its service into an object because, if it does this, it is operating according to the dictates of death instead of life. Accordingly, those who exercise the authority and power Jesus bestows must be moved and influenced by those they seek to influence. Just as Jesus subjected Himself to the influence and control of others and died as a consequence, so those who exercise His authority must risk death—even die—in loving service to others. The power and authority that Jesus bestows, therefore, clearly exclude certain sorts of organizational structures; for some structures are designed to operate under the authority of death rather than life.

It is not that the authority and power Jesus bestows cannot operate within an organization that derives its power and authority from death. Jesus is risen! The power of life is more powerful than the power of death. The power of life can operate in an organization that derives its power from death's authority, but our sins can be used in the service of life only because death now serves life. God can indeed operate in places where death seems to rule. But this fact does not undermine the contention that *the Church* is tempting God when it organizes according to the power and authority of death rather than the power and authority Jesus bestows on His brothers and sisters.

The Church should know better, but it does not seem to act in accord with this knowledge. The fact that we have organized ourselves according to models already present in the world, instead of trying to construct models more consistent with the authority and power Jesus bestows, is almost beyond dispute. In our pronounced tendency to mimic the world, we have also uncritically adopted and employed the world's power. In a post-Constantinian era, however, the bankruptcy of such a course is becoming more and more pronounced. We are beginning to see how we have ignored the poor and the marginalized by our employment of unilateral power. Like the rich man whose daily routine rendered him blind to the very visible Lazarus who suffered and begged at his very gate, our institutional churches have developed routines that exclude the marginalized. This is a consequence of our uncritical adoption of unilateral power; for, unilateral power can safely avoid dealing with those who have no power.[86] In adopting structures that presuppose the use of unilateral power, we make it more likely that the Church's ministry will *not* be done.

This new, post-Constantinian era gives the Church a second chance. Our gracious God has not yet abandoned us to the consequences of our preference for death over life. God has given the Church a second opportunity to organize in such a way that our organization will be more consistent with the power and authority Jesus bestows.

Recognizing that the administrative structures of our churches are not theologically neutral, it is now appropriate to offer some suggestions concerning the Church's organizational patterns in light of our discussions concerning ministry. It must be remembered that the following suggestions are incomplete and should not be taken as definitive. With this important qualification in mind some general patterns of Church structure can be recognized. First, if the Apostle Paul is correct, the Church is an organic unity. Its parts are in a mutual, symbiotic relationship and are not arranged in the one dimensional manner of modern corporations which, on paper at least, are often based on the dictates of unilateral power. The head of the Body of Christ is not unaffected by the heart or the limbs, and the limbs are not unaffected by what happens in the head. The Apostle Paul describes this relationship in this way.

> For the body does not consist of one member but of many. If the foot should say, "Because I am not a hand, I do not belong to the body." And if the ear should say, "Because I am not an eye, I do not belong to the body," that would not make it any less a part of the body. If the whole body were an eye, where would be the hearing? If the whole body were an ear, where would be the sense of smell? But as it is God arranged the organs in the body, each of them, as he chose. If all were a single organ, where would the body be? As it is, there are many parts, yet one body. The eye cannot say to the hand, "I have no need of you," nor again the head to the feet; "I have no need of you." On the contrary, the parts of the body which

> we think less honorable we invest with greater honor, and our unpresentable pasts are treated with greater modesty, which our more presentable parts do not require. But God has so composed the body, giving the greater honor to the inferior part that there may be no discord in the body, but that the members may have the same care for one another. If one member suffers, all suffer together; if one member is honored, all rejoice together. Now you are the body of Christ and individually members of it . . . . [87]

The symbiotic relationship that exists between the members of the Body of Christ is not simply a Pauline construction. It is implied in Matthew in, of all places, Matthew's discussion of what might be called excommunication.

> If your brother sins against you, go and tell him his fault, between you and him alone. If he listens to you, you have gained your brother. But if he does not listen, take one or two others along with you, that every word may be confirmed by the evidence of two or three witnesses. If he refuses to listen to them, tell it to the Church; and if he refuses to listen even to the Church, let him be to you as a Gentile or tax collector. Truly, I say to you, whatever you bind on earth shall be bound in heaven and whatever you loose on earth shall be loosed in heaven. Again I say to you, if two or three of you agree on earth about anything they ask, it will be done for them by my father in heaven. For where two or three are gathered in my name, there am I in the midst of them. [88]

As we have already noted, two things are interesting about this passage. First, the crime that leads to excommunication is not the initial sin. It is not some false doctrine. It is not one well-known immorality or another. The crime is not listening. At first the person does not listen to the one against whom the sin has been committed. Next, there is the refusal to listen to two or three witnesses. Finally, the accused does not listen to the Church. This refusal to listen is very important because it is the same as refusing to be influenced by the brother or sister. (Generally speaking, this is more a crime of theologians, scholars, clerics and those in the hierarchy of the Church, than it is of heretics and others.) Whoever is involved in not listening is also involved in undermining the mutual relations between the members of the Body of Christ. If one organ refuses to be affected by another in this Body, the whole Body suffers.

The second thing to note about this passage is that the one who is cast out is to be treated like a Gentile or tax collector. This is a particularly interesting thing to say in Matthew, "the tax collector's" Gospel. This treatment may well imply that the one removed from this community should not become the object of ridicule and scorn, as might be the case for people removed from other groups. The one dismissed now becomes the purpose of mission; and, since mission is the purpose of the Church in Matthew's Gospel, the value of the one dismissed to the Body of Christ increases. It is, after-all, no accident that Matthew places the parable of the lost sheep immediately before this passage. It is the lost one that is valued by the good shepherd. Readmittance to the Body of Christ can come when the excommunicated one "listens." Readmittance comes when this member not only influences the Body, but is influenced by the body. A clearly mutual and symbiotic relationship exists between the members of the Body.

Both Paul and Matthew, therefore, suggest an organizational structure governed by the power of life that Jesus bestows on His disciples, which emphasizes the symbiotic relationships that should happen between the members of the body. In this organization, no one part is dominated by another. They serve each other. The head does not lord it over the foot. The eye does not make the hand into an object. The power of life is operative here, and this power refuses to turn the living into objects. If such a body is to organize itself, if such a body is to have a written constitution, that constitution must be so designed that it reflects the power and authority of life, not death.

One thing that should be addressed in such organizational designs is the relationship between the ordained and other ministers of God. If we presume death's rule in our constitutional structures and assume that the only sort of power is the power of death, we will design our constitutions in such a way that one group dominates another. If, however, we understand the relationship between ordained and other ministers in terms of the power and authority of life, we can organize in such a way that the symbiotic relationship that ought to exist between all ministers of God is promoted and enhanced by our organizational design.

The Body of Christ can be so organized that our ministries serve each other and are not in conflict with one another. Once again Scripture suggests a pattern where it says, "You know that those who are supposed to rule over the Gentiles lord it over them, and their great men exercise authority over them. But it shall not be so among you; but whoever would be great among you must be your servant, and whoever would be first among you must be slave of all. For the Son of Man also came not to be served, but to serve and to give his life as a ransom for many."[89] In this passage, Jesus is opposing worldly, unilateral power and in so doing, recognizes that his disciples should organize themselves in a different way. In this new organization, the great ones are not to lord it over the rest of the people in the organization. They are to serve. Should such an organization ever contain bishops, the bishops are the ones who are to serve those with less prestige. Should such an organization have pastors or priests, these too are to serve. They do not lord it over those they serve. Should such an organization require teachers, the teachers serve and are not to use their positions to influence and move their students without being open to the influence of their students. Should such an organization have great lay leaders, these leaders are not to lord it over other Christians. They too are to serve. "For the Son of Man also came not to be served, but to serve and to give His life as a ransom to many." It is very possible to organize in such a way that relationships such as these are promoted rather than hindered. It is certainly difficult, but it is possible.

The words "service and love" should characterize the relationship between the ordained and other ministers of God in both theory and practice. Our formal constitutions should attempt to recognize this not simply by paying lip service to this relationship in their preambles, but by instituting concrete formulations that make the embodiment of such relationships more likely. The relationship between the tasks normally associated with the ordained and those normally associated with the priesthood of all believers can easily be understood in terms of mutuality. The tasks normally associated with the ordained support the ministry of the people of God in the world. This relationship is not a one way street, however. Many non-ordained people are called to support the people of God in their many ministries in the world. We have seen that the task of the ordained concerns creating an arena in which the communal task of discerning the presence of Jesus in places Jesus has promised to be present, and that this task is done so that all the gifts present in the community of believers can be brought to bear on the tasks of discernment, witness, and discipleship. It is in the exercise of these gifts—particularly the gifts of wisdom and love—that the lay leadership serves the communion of saints. But, more than this, the relationship between the tasks normally associated with the ordained ministry and those usually associated with the ministries of the people of God are not one dimensional. The tasks of the ordained promote the accomplishment of tasks of the ministries of the priesthood of all believers; likewise, the ministry in the world of the priesthood of all believers are the reason for the very existence of the ordained ministry.

The formal organizational structures of our churches should take the symbiotic relationship between these ministries much more seriously than it does. For years we have structured ourselves so that the people of God help with the tasks that are associated with the ordained. Our formal organizations have done little to support the ministries associated with the people of God. We should eliminate this serious flaw by shaping our structures in such a way as to better support ministries that happen in the world.

That ecclesiastical structure designed to promote ministry in the world would be different from those we currently employ is quite obvious. Many of our local congregations are designed to do only those tasks we normally associate with the ordained. They do not even recognize ministry in the world as a valid expression of discipleship. We are quick to call assisting in worship or working on a church committee ministry, but our ministries in the world are hardly noticed, and more often than not, these ministries go unnoticed, unrecognized, and unsupported by churches that ought to have such ministries as a top priority. Our congregations are generally less likely to be structured to aid the people of God in the more hazardous task of ministry in everyday life.

A simple glance at the typical administrative structure of our congregations is enough to make this point at least plausible. Normally, the more a committee's task is internal to the life of a congregation, the better the committee functions, and the more the committee is concerned with ministries of outreach or vocation-related concerns, the worse it seems to function. The worship committee's task, for example, is generally well defined, but it performs a task normally attributed to the ordained. Even though it is clear that worship has social and political implications that stretch far beyond the internal life of the congregation, worship is seldom interpreted in a way that promotes its relationship to such external things. The education committee also functions pretty well in most churches, even if the Sunday Schools do not. This may be because education is also a task normally attributed to the ordained ministry. The organization of a typical church is pretty good at such tasks. The clergy get a great deal of help with their jobs—as they should. It is not that there is anything wrong with having such committees. The task of discerning the presence of Jesus in places Jesus has promised to be is complex and difficult and should include as many people as possible. The Church should create arenas in which the discernment of Jesus can occur, and committees like worship, education, finance, property, and parish life may well be ways to promote such discernment. The point that is being made here is that these tasks are tasks that are generally attributed to the ordained ministry, and although our congregational structures generally support these tasks quite well, they are less successful in their support of those tasks that are normally associated with ministries of the people of God.

Our difficulties with evangelism, stewardship, and social ministry may well be indicative of our refusal to support the ministries of the whole people of God. These are often problem areas in the life of a congregation because they are tasks that are more concerned with those aspects of congregational life associated with lay ministry. Evangelism involves proclaiming the Gospel message to those who are not of this flock. It is the mission of all congregations! It is our reason for being! It is best accomplished by those whose vocations place them in the world and subject them to the necessities of the world. Yet, many of our congregations have great difficulty with this most important task. Could this difficulty be because we have not organized to support evangelism?

Like evangelism, stewardship is often underdeveloped in our congregations. Normally, we do not understand stewardship as involving our whole lives and our whole planet. Instead, we understand it as raising funds for the congregation, or maybe offering our time and talents to ministries that are normally associated with the ordained. Very little is said about our stewardship of the planet. That would involve us too deeply in social and political issues, and, until we bridge the gap between Sunday and Monday, such issues will mistakenly be viewed as outside the realm of our ministries. It is when stewardship begins to address issues not directly associated with the congregation's inner life that it has a tendency to flounder. Yet, these are clearly tasks normally associated with the priesthood of all believers. The present state of affairs will prevail as long as we continue to organize according to the dictates of death, for the power and authority of death divides, separates and objectifies. It has clearly done so in the case of stewardship. By confining stewardship to tasks of the ordained, we have undermined our very purpose for being in the world. We are here to be agents of life. Our allegiance to death's rule prevents us from employing the power of life in the world. Death's power has been successful at separating our Church stewardship from stewardship of the planet. It need not be so, but it is so, because we insist on organizing according to death's dictates.

Finally, social ministry is often administratively troublesome because there are hazards to social ministry that are quite comparable to the hazards involved in the ministries of the people of God. Social ministry often forces individual congregations to choose between necessities imposed on them by their need to survive, and their Lord—who might be calling them to abandon their pursuit of money, power and property.

Congregations as well as individuals find themselves losing their lives in order to find them. In any case, a congregation's demise is not as important as its attempt to be faithful to its Lord. If a congregation's neighborhood, community, city, or nation proves to be its cross, then that cross should not be abandoned in favor of self perpetuation.

In spite of these difficulties, stewardship, evangelism and social ministry are done very well by some congregations that have begun to understand ministry in terms of the whole people of God rather than in terms of tasks normally associated with the ordained ministry. Even in such congregations, however, there may be little recognition and support for the activities of the people of God as they try to minister in everyday life. There are very few groups established to support Christians as they seek to discern Jesus' presence, to witness, and to follow Jesus in places that Jesus has not promised to be but is present nonetheless. There are few opportunities to come together and discuss how to live like a Christian at home, on the job, or in the community. In most cases, a committed Christian has nowhere to turn when faced with the difficult and hazardous task of being a Christian in a world that is often hostile to Jesus. If the ministries of the people of God are not intentionally supported and publicly recognized in the structure and life of the congregation, these ministries run the risk of perishing. They have not yet perished, but unless the ministry of the whole people of God is supported by the formal structures of our congregations, the ministry of the people of God is in jeopardy.[90]

Some have rightly said that Word, Sacraments, and prayers have always supported the ministry of the whole people of God, but a more intentional support of these important ministries would give us more to address in our sermons and more to pray about in our prayers. In not supporting the ministries of the people of God within the organization of our congregations, we run the risk of divorcing daily life from the very rituals that give vitality to daily life.

When the author of Ephesians exhorts us to put on the whole armor of Christ, he or she recommends girding one's loins with truth, putting on the breastplate of righteousness, wearing the gospel of peace for shoes, protecting ourselves with the shield of faith, wearing the helmet of salvation and using prayer and the sword of the Spirit.[91] These are recommended because "we are not contending against flesh and blood, but against the world rulers of this present darkness, against the spiritual host of wickedness in heavenly places." In other words, there is a purpose for worship and those exercises we normally associate with the spiritual life. The purpose is to do battle in the world against powers that are not merely human. It is to engage the necessities imposed by the context into which a person is called, and prevail by using the armor of God. We only can prevail using this armor, but if we wear this spiritual armor and do not fight the battle, it not only looks funny but it simply becomes a cumbersome relic of past crusades. It is tough to walk around in armor all day, particularly if it is not being used for anything in particular. This fact alone might help explain the boring nature of much of our worship life. Worship that does not support our lives in the world tends to become boring and dull. As long as this world remains, a spiritual life without a battle is ridiculous.

The Church should structure itself in such a way that it more intentionally supports the priesthood of all believers in its ministry in the world. It should gather groups of believers to discuss the joys, sorrows and temptations associated with ministry in the world. Groups like this are necessary, because the ministries of God's people often take place where communal support for these difficult ministries is not immediately available. Those who discern, witness, and follow Jesus in media in which Jesus has not promised to be but goes nonetheless often do not know where to begin looking for Jesus. Groups that intentionally gather to support people engaged in such ministry can help. Such groups can provide ideas for new places to look for Jesus. They can be a source of support in times of temptation, and they can inspire and direct those who feel isolated in their ministries.

An organizational pattern that supports the ministries of the people of God need not be limited to support groups. Congregations, regional and national church bodies could provide some financial support. Money could easily be set aside to support those who get into trouble *because* they are disciples of Jesus in the world. A person could lose a job because of his or her attempt to minister, and our church bodies should try to support such people. The fact that we only pay the ordained, and others who attend to the internal dynamics of the church, should be reexamined in light of the vital importance of the ministry of the people of God in the world.

Our administrative structures themselves must recognize the symbiotic relationship that exists between all of the

Church's ministries. In doing so, our structures will more closely resemble an organic body than the modern corporations that they currently mimic. The gifts of the whole body ought to be brought to bear on the discernment of the precise structures that might aid us in this task. This being done, the way we organize ourselves would be a little more consistent with the Gospel we proclaim.

FROM SUNDAY TO MONDAY

It is often said that the ministry of the whole people of God depends on our ability to translate what happens on Sunday into action on Monday, and, increasingly, this translation is becoming more and more difficult. A growing number of Christians see no relationship between what happens on Sunday and their everyday lives. This problem, too, may be the result of our preference for the power and authority of death; for, as long as we compartmentalize and rank our ministries, one group of ministers will dominate. Currently, it seems that the ordained ministers dominate at least our understanding of what ministry is. For some reason it is easy for us to see that the tasks we normally associate with the ordained are ministry. Indeed, we often identify these tasks with ministry and exclude other more mundane activities from our discussions on ministry, and if these mundane activities are excluded from our discussion, Christianity itself is in trouble because we spend most of our time doing these everyday things.

This difficulty is all the more tragic because, in principle at least, there is no difference between the ministries of the ordained and the ministries of the people of God. In other words, there is no need to make "translations" from Sunday to Monday. Our Sundays' ministries involve the discernment, witness, and following of Jesus in media where Jesus has promised to be present. Our Mondays' ministries involved the discernment, witness, and following of Jesus in media in which he has not promised to be present, but may be present nonetheless. Both sorts of ministries involve the discernment, witness, and following of Jesus. Both sorts of ministries are the same—at least in principle.

What distinguishes those ministries we normally associate with the ordained from those we normally associate with the people of God is the context in which discernment, witness and discipleship take place. It is one thing to minister in the safe confines of a North American mainline congregation. It is another to minister in the world of high finance or as a cashier in a department store. The context dictates the activity of a particular minister, but the vocation of all people of God is to discern, to witness and to follow Jesus in these different contexts.

Our preference for the power and authority of death has often prevented us from understanding the close relationship between the ministries of the ordained and the ministries of the whole people of God. In assuming the primacy of death, we have isolated one ministry from another. Indeed, we have tended to subjugate one ministry to the other. From time to time the ordained have dominated. More rarely, the priesthood of all believers has dominated. This sad state of affairs will continue as long as we prefer the authority of death to the authority and power of life. Since the only question is, "Who is going to dominate whom?" we have difficulty in understanding the relationship between Sunday and Monday. As long as one group dominates another, ministry will be understood solely in terms of the dominant group. The other group will have value only in so far as it ignores its own tasks and does those tasks of the dominant group. Under such circumstances, it is no wonder that many have trouble relating Sunday to Monday. If ministry is defined strictly in terms of Sunday, ministry will be impossible on Monday and vice versa. The authority and power of death establishes such divisions.

It is simply not necessary to continue in this way. If we understand our lives and our ministries against the background of the authority and power that Jesus bestows, it will be possible to understand and do many things differently. In this presentation, new possibilities for ministry have been suggested. We have seen that a symbiotic relationship between ministries is quite possible. We have seen how the ministries we normally associate with the ordained can support ministries we often associate with the laity. We have recognized the need for corporate discernment so that all the gifts of the Spirit can be brought to bear on the critical task of discernment, and we have shown how it is possible to organize so that the activities of the people of God can be better supported. The key to such support and mutuality is the utilization of the power and authority that Jesus bestows on His followers. This power does not lead to division. It leads to mutuality. Mutuality is never easy to accomplish, but it can be accomplished because it is consistent with the Lord of Life.

Notes

INTRODUCTION

[1]Understanding forgiveness as refusing to insist on one's rights is not intended to recover a Biblical definition of forgiveness *per se*. It is intended to describe the spirit of the word forgiveness in a modern context. The day will probably come when we do not equate our lives with our rights. When that day comes, forgiveness will have to be described in another way.

[2]Mark 9: 33-37 is illustrative of this point as are its parallels Matthew 18: 1-5 and Luke 9: 46-48.

[3]It was the reformers who interpreted the medieval Christian doctrine of ordination as bestowing a substantial or ontological change on the one who is ordained.

THE CHURCH IN THE WORLD

[4]That the Church depends on Jesus' presence and that it depends on the Word of God are the same thing. Jesus is the Word which became flesh and dwelt among us. The ecclesiology here presented, then, is Word-oriented because it is Jesus-oriented.

[5]Matthew 13: 44-46.

[6]John 1: 19ff.

[7]Gregory of Nyssa, *The Life of Moses* 253, 254 in *The Classics of Western Spirituality*, translated by Abraham J. Malherbe and Everett Ferguson (New York: Paulist Press, 1978) p. 120.

[8]"The Augsburg Confession," Article VII, *The Book of Concord: The Confessions of the Evangelical Lutheran Church*, translated and edited by Theodore G. Tappert (Philadelphia: Fortress Press, 1959) p. 32.

[9]One way to hold that the Augsburg Confession and some other confessional documents actually do give a complete description of the Church is to expand the notion of sacrament to include any medium in which Jesus promises to be present. Understood in this way, the possible media where Jesus has promised to be that are to be described are also candidates for sacraments as well.

[10]The followers of Zwingli have correctly pointed out that the danger of idolatry exists for those who might assume Jesus' real presence in the Supper, but this is the case only if the Supper ceases to be a medium in which Jesus is present and becomes Jesus Himself. It must be stressed that Jesus is not synonymous with the media in which He presents Himself. When this is not stressed, there is always the danger of idolatry. The danger becomes very real whenever the Supper is not considered a medium. As long as it is remembered that a medium only presents Jesus and that it is not Jesus, the danger of idolatry can be combatted.

[11]Matthew 28: 18-20

[12]In commenting on Harvey Cox, *Many Mansions* (Boston: Beacon Press, 1988), p. 8, 9; Carl E. Braaten recognizes one of his quite uncharacteristic agreements with Cox when he notes, " . . . people of other faiths want to hear about Jesus, who is much more interesting than some abstract belief in a super-essential something or other beyond all predications." Cox says that from his experience—and he has a lot of it—the Jesus factor is surprisingly just what the non-Christian participants in dialogue are most interested in and most eager to talk about. Cox candidly confesses, "I too tried to avoid talking about Jesus too quickly, but I soon discovered my interlocutors wanted to." Carl E. Braaten, "Preaching Christ in an Age of Religious Pluralism," *World and Word*, Vol. IX, No. 3, Summer 1989, p. 245.

[13]Isaiah 55: 10, 11.

[14]For insight into the type of power that is implicit in conversation, I am in the debt of Peter J. Paris, *The Social Teachings of the Black Churches* (Philadelphia: Fortress Press, 1985) p. 114-125, and Dr. Paris says that his observations are in debt to Bernard Loomer, "Two Kinds of Power," *Criterion*, 15, no. 1 (Winter 1976) p.

12-29. The issue of the type of power that is referred to here will be discussed in more detail in Chapter III.

[15]Bodies need not be interpreted as being fundamentally matter even though they clearly contain matter. Modern physics seems to suggest that a body may be, more fundamentally, the power to gather matter. As such, bodies are more fundamentally a power or relationship than they are matter. Discerning Jesus' body, therefore, involves discerning His power and His relationships within the media in which Jesus has promised to be present. It will probably be discovered that the Jesus we discern in our midst has much the same relationship to us as He did to His disciples.

[16]Robert W. Jenson, *Visible Words* (Philadelphia Fortress Press.) pp. 28-50.

THE TASK AND CHARISM OF THE ORDAINED MINISTRY

[17]See introduction note 3.

[18]*Dictionary of Behavioral Science*, Compiled and edited by Benjamin B. Wolman (New York: Van Nostrand Reinhold Company, 1973) p. 390.

[19]*Ibid.*

[20]Gregory of Nyssa, "To Ablabius: 'On Not Three Gods,' " in *Selected Writings and Letters of Gregory of Nyssa*, translated by William More, *Nicene and Post-Nicene Fathers*, Second Series, Vol. V (Grand Rapids, Michigan: Wm. B. Eerdmans Publishing Company, 1954) p. 334.

[21]I Timothy 4: 11-16.

[22]*Ibid.*

[23]Martin Dibelius and Hans Conzelmann, *The Pastoral Epistles*, translated by Philip Buttolph and Adela Yarbro (Philadelphia: Fortress Press, 1972) p. 71.

[24]Hans Conzelmann and Walther Zimmerli, "*charisma*," *Theological Dictionary of the New Testament*: Vol. IX, edited by Gerhard Friedrich, translated by Geoffrey W. Bromiley (Grand Rapids, Michigan: Wm. B. Eerdmans Publishing Co., 1974) p. 403.

[25]Hans Conzelmann and Walther Zimmerli, *"charis," Ibid.*, p. 394.

[26]*Ibid.*

[27]*Ibid.*, p. 398.

[28]Hans Conzelmann and Walther Zimmerli, *"charisma," Ibid.*, p. 404.

[29]Walter Foerster, *"exousia," The Theological Dictionary of the New Testament*, Vol. II, p. 568, 569.

[30]*Ibid.*, p. 566.

[31]Enrique D. Dussell, *A History of the Church in Latin America: Colonialism to Liberation (1492-1979)*, translated and revised by Alan Neely (Grand Rapids Michigan: William B. Eerdmans Publishing Co., 1981) p. 47-71.

[32]Nena and George O'Neill, *Shifting Gears: Finding Security in a Changing World* (New York: Avon Books, 1975) p.17, describe a crisis as follows: "The assumptions with which we begin, whatever they may be, comprise our assumptive state. When our assumptive state is challenged, we are in crisis."

[33]Robert C. Gregg and Dennis E. Groh, *Early Arianism: A View of Salvation* (Philadelphia: Fortress Press, 1981) p. 260-274.

[34]Athanasius, *On the Incarnation in Nicene and Post-Nicene Father*, Series 2, Vol. IV, p. 40.

[35]Gregory of Nyssa, "To Ablabius: On Not Three Gods." *Nicene and Post-Nicene Fathers*, Second Series, Vol. V, p. 334.

[36]I Corinthians 13: 13.

PASTORAL AUTHORITY

[37]Terrence E. Fretheim, *The Suffering of God: An Old Testament Perspective* (Philadelphia: Fortress Press, 1984) p. 60-79.

[38]*Ibid.*, p. 61.

[39]*Ibid.*, p. 62.

[40]Robert W. Jenson, *The Triune Identity: God According to the Gospel* (Philadelphia: Fortress Press, 1982) p. 33-40.

[41]Genesis 15: 7-11,17.

[42]Foster McCurley and John Reuman, *Witness of the Word: A Biblical Theology of the Gospel* (Philadelphia: Fortress Press, 1986) p. 165, 166.

[43]Fretheim, p. 66.

[44]Martin Luther, "Lectures on Galatians. 1535," translated by Jaroslav Pelikan in *Luther's Works,* Vol. 26 (St. Louis: Concordia Publishing House, 1963) p. 277. Hereafter this edition of Luther's Works will be abbreviated L. W. In any case, the argument that follows is based upon and derived from Gerhard Forde, "The Work of Christ," in *Christian Dogmatics,* Vol. 2, edited by Carl E. Braaten and Robert W. Jenson (Philadelphia: Fortress Press, 1984) p. 47-98.

[45]Martin Hengel, *Crucifixion* (Philadelphia: Fortress Press, 1977) p. 33.

[46]*Ibid.*, p. 34.

[47]*Ibid.*, p. 51.

[48]Juvenal 6.219ff. as quoted, Hengel, p. 57, 58.

[49]Ernst Kasemann, *Perspectives on Paul,* translated by Margaret Kuhl (Philadelphia: Fortress Press, 1971) p. 36.

[50]Luther, "Lectures on Galatians. 1535," in *L.W.*, Vol. 26, p. 277.

[51]Even our hospitals tend to become centers that reinforce the idea that death is the exception, and that it is only an individual affair. We often die in isolated rooms abandoned by doctors who can "do no more." Even our loved ones are sometimes encouraged to leave. After all, we are told, what more can we do. In any case, this situation serves the ideology of the masters who can maintain the illusion that they control the future. Such an illusion can only be accomplished if the fact of death is denied.

[52]John 13: 12-16.

[53]Mark 10: 35-45.

[54]*Webster's New World Dictionary of the American Language: College Edition,* edited by David B. Guralnik and Joseph H. Friend (New York: The World Publishing Company, 1964) p. 1145.

[55]Peter J. Paris, *The Social Teaching of the Black Churches* (Philadelphia: Fortress Press, 1985) p. 113, 114.

[56]Bernard Loomer, "Two Kinds of Power," *Criterion* 15, no. 1. (Winter, 1976) p. 12-29.

[57]*Ibid.*, p. 14.

[58]*Ibid.*, p. 16.

[59]Paris, p. 114.

[60]"Augsburg Confession," Article 28, *Book of Concord*, p. 82.

[61]Paris, p. 115.

[62]*Ibid.*, p. 118.

[63]*Ibid.*, p. 118.

[64]Romans 6: 3-4.

[65]Raine Eisler, *The Chalice and the Blade* (San Francisco: Harper and Row, 1988).

[66]*Ibid.*, p. xvii.

[67]*Ibid.*, p. 1-103.

[68]*Ibid.*, p. xvi, xvii

[69]Mark 10: 13ff.

[70]Mark 9: 33-37.

[71]The word "refusal" may be too kind a word to use in this context. It is probably more accurate to say that it never occurred to us to ordain women. This is even a more grave sin.

[72]Jacques Ellul, *The Subversion of Christianity*, translated by Geoffrey W. Bromiley (Grand Rapids, Michigan: William B. Eerdmans Publishing Company, 1986).

[73]*Ibid.*, p. 33, 34.

[74]Dorothee Soelle makes a similar but much more extensive argument concerning the same point in *The Strength of the Weak: Toward a Christian Feminist Identity*, translated by Robert and Rita Kimber (Philadelphia: The Westminster Press, 1984).

[75]This assertion may sound strange coming from someone who claims to be in the Lutheran tradition, because we claim that the Word of God is a Word of both Law and Gospel, and that temporal authorities rely on the authority of law (civil use of the law) in order to govern. It must be remembered, however, that the Law is closely associated with death in such thinking. While Lutherans assert that

the civil use of the Law can be summarized as God using sin against sin to create a realm of relative peace, it is clear that the civil realm's ultimate ability to kill is one authority on which this ability rests. Indeed, it might be argued that we can use sin against sin to create a realm of relative peace only because the authority of life has triumphed over death, and, as such, death is at life's disposal.

[76]Bonnie Bowman Thurston, *The Widows: A Women's Ministry in The Early Church* (Minneapolis: Fortress Press, 1989) p. 7, 8.

[77]See Alice L. Laffey, *An Introduction to the Old Testament: A Feminist Perspective* (Philadelphia: Fortress Press, 1988) as indicative of the conscious or subconscious attempts on the part of patriarchal culture to minimize the roles of women in the Old Testament.

[78]Exodus 1:15-2:10.

[79]Laffey, p. 47.

[80]Thurston, p. 44 and 45.

THE PRIESTHOOD OF ALL BELIEVERS

[81]See introduction.

[82]Jacques Ellul, *The Ethics of Freedom*, translated and edited by Geoffrey W. Bromiley (Grand Rapids, Michigan: William B. Eerdmans Publishing Company, 1976) p. 37-50.

[83]Our Christmas preparations have remarkable similarities to the five-day Babylonian ritual of reviving their God Marduk. According to Babylonian myth, before time began, Marduk fought the leviathan Tiamat and won. Out of the dead serpent's body, Marduk formed the earth and populated it. The only trouble with the earth was that it was made from the body of Tiamat, and every year that fact had an influence on the earth's creativity. Due to nature's regular cycles, there came a time each year when crops would not grow. What was needed was Marduk to once again slay Tiamat who once again seemed to be rearing his ugly head. The Babylonians, however, knew what to do. They ritualistically reenacted Tiamat's slaying in the hope that Marduk would wake up and take part in this ritual. Evidently, the ritual worked because, shortly after this yearly ritual, the earth would once again yield its

fruits. The Babylonians had revived their god, and Marduk was once again on guard, at least until he would rest once again about the same time next year. We moderns tend to laugh at such rituals as this until we note that, at least in the United States, we perform the same sort of ritual only ours takes about thirty days where the Babylonian ritual took only five. Every year on the day after Thanksgiving, little fat men in red suits descend on every shopping center in the nation, and our citizens pack themselves into stores to begin a thirty-day ritual of buying. All during this frenzy, our newspapers, radios, and televisions have people called economists, who argue about one fundamental question, "Will this Christmas buying activity be enough to revive the Economy?" As the Babylonians tried to revive their god, we try to revive ours. The only difference is that our god—the god we name Economy—is a little more difficult to wake up. It takes us thirty days. The Babylonians only took five.

[84]Neil Postman, *Amusing Ourselves to Death: Public Discourse in the Age of Show Business* (New York: Penguin Books, 1985) p. 7.

[85]Matthew 10: 33ff.

[86]Many Christians refrain from serious discussion of the organizational structure of churches because they contend that such structures are adiaphora or not essential. While it is true that a particular organizational structure may be adiaphora, and while it is true that there are many ways to organize our corporate life, this does not mean that church structure is not important. Because Jesus is essential to the life of the church, it is important to organize in such a way that our organizational structure testifies to Jesus' central status. Because this can be done in a number of ways, the structure is adiaphora, but because it cannot be done by any willy nilly organization, how we structure ourselves is an important issue.

[87]I Corinthians 12: 14-27a.

[88]Matthew 18: 15-20.

[89]Mark 10: 35-45.

[90]Although our current structures place the ministry of the people of God in jeopardy, people have recently begun to recognize the absolute necessity of such ministries. A pioneer in such discussions is Nelvin Vos. His contributions include, *Monday's*

Ministries: The Ministry of the Laity, edited by Raymond Tiemeyer (Philadelphia: Parish Life Press, 1979) and *Seven Days a Week: Faith in Action* (Philadelphia: Fortress Press, 1985). See also the work of William E. Diehl, *Christianity In Real Life* (Philadelphia: Fortress Press, 1976) and *The Monday Connection: A Spirituality of Competence, Affirmation and Support In The Workplace* (San Francisco: Harper, 1991).

[91]Ephesians 6: 11-18.

To order additional copies of this book, please use coupon below.

Mail to:

Brunswick Publishing Corporation
ROUTE 1, BOX 1-A-1
LAWRENCEVILLE, VIRGINIA 23868

Order Form

Please send me ______ copy(s) of *Ministry with the Power of Jesus,* by Dr. Scott W. Gustafson, ISBN 1-55618-105-1, LC 91-72232, at $14.95 per copy plus $3.50 mailing and handling. Virginia residents add 4.5% (67¢) sales tax.

☐ Check enclosed. Charge Orders — 804-848-3865

☐ Charge to my credit card: ☐ VISA ☐ MasterCard

Card # ______________________________ Exp. Date __________

Signature: ______________________________

Name ______________________________

Address ______________________________

City ____________________ State ______ Zip__________

Phone # ______________________________